EXAMINATION OF "WIDESPREAD CITIZEN PARTICIPATION" IN THE MODEL CITIES PROGRAM AND THE DEMANDS OF ETHNIC MINORITIES FOR A GREATER DECISION MAKING ROLE IN AMERICAN CITIES

RICARDO A. MILLETT

San Francisco, California
1977

Published by

R & E RESEARCH ASSOCIATES, INC.
4843 Mission Street
San Francisco, California 94112

Publishers
Robert D. Reed and Adam S. Eterovich

Library of Congress Card Catalog Number

76-56556

I.S.B.N.
0-88247-445-6

TABLE OF CONTENTS

iii

INTRODUCTION

This study focuses on three major areas of research interest in the Model Cities Program: descriptive, evaluative and analytical.

a) Descriptively, the study represents an attempt to describe and explain the Model Cities Program as a federal intervention in the social, political and economic problems of the urban poor.

b) It is evaluative in that it raises questions as to the operational effectiveness of the program's participatory mechanisms designed to channel and structure the rising demands of ethnic minorities for a greater role in urban decision-making as such decisions affect their lives.

c) It is analytical in that it employs the tools of empirical research methodology to analyze some of the factors and conditions which are correlated with resident participation in eleven urban localities.

The Model Cities Program is the most comprehensively developed program of the Department of Housing and Urban Development to respond to the needs of the urban poor. The underlying strategy of the program assumes that physical revitalization of low-income neighborhoods is inadequate unless appropriate action is also taken to ameliorate the social and economic problems which accompany deteriorating buildings and facilities. The program has also attempted to coordinate federal, state, and local, as well as private resources as a means to increase the effectiveness of the attack on poverty. Finally, the Program recognizes that the participation of neighborhood residents in developing local programs is essential to success. Although the mandate for resident participation is contained in the program statute, the development of a workable arrangement for the operationalization of "widespread citizen participation" is left in large measure to the urban locality.

With respect to the latter, resident participation in the Model Cities Program represents a retreat from "resident participation" as it was practiced in Community Action Programs (CAP). Resident participation in the CAP took place in private, non-profit, non-governmental agencies. The OEO legislation containing the guidelines for CAP provided an option whereby local governments could delegate the authority to operate the program to agencies outside of its political hegemony. In fact, most of the CAP programs (95%) were operated by non-governmental agencies.[1] This arrangement later stimulated considerable controversy around the issue of resident participation in the CAP program. The Model Cities program, on the other hand, places ultimate authority for the program with the elected officials of the urban locality. Although section 103 of the Demonstration City and Metropolitan Development Act of 1966 stipulates that there must be "widespread citizen participation in the program," private non-profit organizations such as those which administered the community action organizations were not allowed.

Some students of the "participation" issue have viewed the provisions for resident participation in the Model Cities program as a conscious attempt to decrease the concern with and emphasis on resident participation -- particularly where "resident" is interpreted as ethnic minorities.[2] Elsewhere this de-emphasis has been identified with the ghetto rebellions of the 1960's and the increased political awareness of ethnic minorities during this period.[3] Against these observations the Model Cities Program merits special consideration. If indeed the federal response to the needs of the urban poor was to develop a program counter to OEO (which had become identified as an advocate for the poor), what effect did this effort have on the activities of ethnic minorities to become legitimate participants in the political process? From the perspective of the "powerless" of the American slums, the program could become responsive and meaningful only to the extent that they could seize the opportunities the Program offers and make it serve the needs of their community. However, the frustrations of ethnic minorities with the inability and/or unwillingness of social institutions to respond to their needs led them to believe that they must control some part of any program allegedly designed to help them. In the Model Cities program, "resident participation" from this perspective, can be workable only with such control, while retaining the support of the local chief executive and the heads of important governmental agencies. As Ralph Taylor stated:

> "Beneath the rhetoric, however, there can be no exclusive
> control by citizens or by any single citizen group. The
> work that has to be done can be accomplished only by the
> various public and private forces working together. In
> the Model Cities Program the responsibility for marshall-
> ing the public and private forces through political leader-
> ship is placed on the Chief Executive of local government."[4]

Essentially, therefore, the character and extent of resident participation depends in large measure on the particular social, economic and political dynamics in the urban locality where a Model Cities Program is operationalized.

This study is an attempt to identify some of the more significant factors and conditions which were associated with the particular level of "participation" attained by Model Neighborhood residents in eleven Model Cities Programs. It is hoped that such an analysis will provide some answers to questions concerning the responsiveness of national intervention programs to the needs of the urban ethnic poor (with whom these programs have become identified).

The overall concern of the study, then, is to examine the issues of participation from the vantage point of the "have-nots" in this society, with particular emphasis on the black perspective. The experience of black people in the United States is, of course, not to be totally identified with that of other ethnic minorities. Yet it is hardly debatable that of all the national and racial minorities in this country, Afro-Americans, American-Indians and Spanish surname citizens (Mexican-Americans, Puerto Ricans and other Latin ethnics) have suffered the most racial discrimination and have had least access to the larger American community. From the black perspective, black America exists in a state of social, economic and political subordination to white America. From a political viewpoint these circumstances define black America's "underdevelopment" as a nation and highlights the fact that the more important political decisions in black communities are made by whites outside the black community.

It could be argued that ethnic minorities view the "participation" requirements in intervention programs as an opportunity to rid themselves of the political "powerlessness" which has excluded them from their equal share of goods, benefits, and status in American society. "Resident participation" has to be understood within the historical struggles of ethnic minorities to better their lot in American society. One of the more recent manifestations of this struggle is the black power "movement". The underlying philosophy of this "movement" calls for an increase in the economic and political power of ethnic minorities under the banner of "community control". These two goals represent the essential thrust of "resident participation" from the perspective of ethnic minorities. They are aimed at increasing ethnic minorities' ability and right to have more input than they now have in governing their own destiny.

The Model Cities planning effort, in so far as it attempts to integrate "widespread citizen participation" in its operational process, is a recognition of the need to provide participatory mechanisms for targeted communities. However, the controversies surrounding "resident participation" as

3

operationalized in the CAPs coupled with the apparent de-emphasis on "resident participation" in Model Cities, raises the question of the effectiveness of federal provisions for resident participation in meeting the needs of the "powerless" for increased roles in the decision-making processes which affect their lives.

How, then, is "widespread citizen participation" unfolding in the ghettoes of urban areas? How does the decision-making processes which have evolved in the Model Cities Program relate to the ethnic minorities' demands for increased influence in decision-making? Specifically, have ethnic minority groups been able to use the participation mechanisms in the Model Cities Program to resolve their sense of powerlessness? And if so, under what conditions?

These are some of the questions which need to be answered if intervention efforts like Model Cities are to address themselves to the inaccessibility of ethnic minorities to the network of decisions which directly affect their lives.

For an issue of such current importance, there has been little attempt to coordinate data useful to ethnic minority groups in planning for a more effective decision-making role in their communities. This dissertation, then, has a dual thrust: to examine on the one hand the activities of residents to gain a significant role in the decision-making process of Model Cities; and on the other, to examine the local urban administrative response to these activities.

My bias is that I firmly believe in the demands for greater participation that ethnic minorities are trying to realize. My approach, however, is to analyze and criticize, for only in this way will a useable body of knowledge be built on the subject.

Footnotes - Introduction:

1. John Strange, "The Impact of Citizen Participation on Public Administration," in Public Administration Review (Special Issue); Vol. XXXII, September, 1972, p. 462.

2. Melvin Mogoluf considers this possibility in his paper: Citizen Participation: "A Review and Commentary on Federal Policies and Practices," (Washington, D.C., The Urban Institute, 1970) mimeo; Part I, pp. 75-82. Also see John Strange, ibid., p. 464 -- Also Roland Warren, "The Model Cities Program: Assumptions - Experiences - Implications," paper presented at the Annual Forum Program, National Conference on Social Welfare, Dallas, Texas, May 17, 1971.

3. See for example, Frances Fox Riven and Richard A. Cloward, Regulating the Poor; The Functions of Public Welfare, Chapter 9; also Samuel Yette, The Choice: The Issue of Black Survival in America, Chapter I. Both of these books provide very convincing arguments in support of this proposition.

4. Hans, B. C., Spiegel (editor), Citizen Participation in Urban Government, Vol. II, National Institute for Applied Behavioral Science, Washington, D. C., p. 107.

BRIEF HISTORICAL SURVEY OF CITIZEN PARTICIPATION
IN FEDERAL INTERVENTION PROGRAMS

A significant aspect of the Model Cities program is its call for "Widespread Citizen Participation". However, the vagueness of this language has caused both local residents and officials to ask: What is intended by this requirement, and how will participation be measured? What does the phrase "citizen participation" mean in the first place? There is considerable confusion among the various actors involved in all programs to date which, like the Model Cities Program, have set forth this requirement.

During the 1950's, the phrase was defined essentially as public relations or blue ribbon committees of volunteers or appointees who met, on occasion, with public officials. With the exception of a small number of agricultural and conservation programs, committees of this sort wielded no power; indeed, their members sought neither influence nor control over the programs in which they nominally participated.

In an effort to trace the historical development of "citizen participation," David Austin (1970) notes that it has taken three forms.[1]

1. Egalitarian Democracy: The form of citizen participation arose in principle and form as members of the newly founded American government demanded that "democratic elitism" give way to a more representative decision-making process. This inherent form of "egalitarian democracy" and its principles are a cornerstone of the constitutional provisions for referendums and for recall elections which were adapted by numerous states in the early 1900's. Spin-offs of the principle were used as the basis of political actions to enforce the "one-man-one-vote principle in balloting for public offices and to extend the decentralization of public administration in order to "keep government close to the people."

2. Participation as an advocate position for equal employment: This form of the participation demand can be traced back to Andrew Jackson and the political spoils system of the 1800's. Essentially, it is a demand which takes the position of equal access among all citizens for public employment. The contemporary

character of this demand is seen in the desire on the part of some community advocate groups to have their members rather than outsiders operate "social intervention programs in their communities."

3. Participation as a Vehicle of Control: This form of citizen participation is the approach generally assumed by ethnic minority groups who link this issue with their objective political condition. It is seen as an exercise with some potential to increase their "political efficiency," i.e., a call for some measure of control of the decision inputs and the service and resource outputs of those public institutions and public offices directly affecting the welfare of their communities. A re-occuring issue in this form of "citizen participation" is the replacement of those previously established leaders who are not of the same interest group by the leaders who are indigenous to the population being directly affected by these institutions or offices.

During the 1960's, the phrase "citizen participation" came to signify the latter. The political education of the poor stimulated by the Civil Rights Movement and the War on Poverty changed the content of the phrase for both citizens and public officials. Citizens who had suffered for generations from the effects of exploitation, exclusion, and poverty found new dignity, ambition, and hope through participation in planning and implementing public programs. The social and political condition of minority groups in American society has prompted attempts for a more egalitarian democratic process, a more active and influential role in decision-making bodies, and increasingly, for more influence in implementation of decisions at the institutional level. Sherri Arnstein's definition of what constitutes "citizen participation" integrates these issues in a single term: "citizen power". She writes:[2]

> "My answer to the critical 'what' question is simply that citizen participation is a categorical term for citizen power. It is the redistribution of power that enables the 'have-not' citizens, presently excluded from the political and economic process, to be deliberately included in the future. It is the strategy by which the have-nots join in determining how information is shared, goals and policies are set, tax resources are allocated, programs operated, and benefits like contracts and patronage are parcelled out. In short, it is the means by which they can induce significant social reform which enables them to share in

the benefits of the affluent society."

For Arnstein, the essential and fundamental issue in the whole question of participation is the redistribution of power; a change in the present pattern of power relationships in our society so that the "have-nots" will have more influence than they now command to make social institutions responsive to their objective condition. Indeed, for the majority of ethnic minority residents who have had occasion to be active in participatory processes, power redistribution is paramount. William Bethea, Executive Director of the Northeast Model Cities Citizen's Union, has stated:[3]

> "My own definition is very simple. First, citizens, when I
> talk about citizens, I mean those men, women and youth who
> have traditionally been excluded from the halls - and more
> important, the inner offices of power: the black, the
> brown, the Spanish speaking and the disenfranchised whites...
> The important question is who gets what share of the pie as
> a result of participation. Bankers, real estate interest,
> the medical and social service establishment, and others of
> the locally powerful always have and still do participate.
> They have also received the benefits of that participation
> process. The locally powerful do one other thing that is
> essential to understanding my definition of participation
> to close the circle so that those outside cannot get inside.
> Further, they dole out the benefits in a manner that neither
> threatens them nor permits too much to be given away outside
> the circle. Citizen participation has not only been around,
> I would say it worked very well indeed - for the few. So
> what is my definition of the new participation? It comes
> down to a redistribution of funds and services and providing
> the mechanisms to promote this in our urban communities."

Regardless of what forms the issue of "citizen participation" has taken in the past, it is becoming increasingly evident that the main thrust is that of increasing the "power" of the "powerless".[4] The concern of citizen participation in the earlier years of federal intervention programs was whether and to what extent citizens were to be included in the planning, operation and delivery of social services. Today, the substantive issues inherent in Arnstein's and Bethea's definition of citizen participation are not only becoming popular but represent an insistent demand on the part of the "have-nots" in an affluent society. From this perspective, "citizen participation" can be seen as coterminous with "community control" and the decentralization of decision-making powers from those bodies and institutions who have traditionally held them to those to whom they have been traditionally denied.

The transition from volunteerism and blue ribbon committees to "maximum feasible participation" and "widespread citizen participation" has been marked with such controversy that it has had repercussions both in the practical and theoretical spheres of the social sciences. Various interpretations and attempted operationalizations of the term have stimulated heated political debates and heightened national anxiety. Despite this it seems that "citizen participation" is here to stay.[5] The critical question then becomes: in what form will it be accepted; and will its accepted form be the most effective? If not, what other form of social innovation will attempt to ensure the inputs of the "have-nots" in resource allocation as it affects them?

Insights into the possible answers to these questions can be discerned from the experience of "citizen participation" as it emerged from the Gray Areas Projects, Mobilization for Youth Program, the Community Action Program, and finally the Model Cities Program. This evolution has been described and analyzed by Daniel P. Moynihan in "Maximum Feasible Misunderstanding" (1969) and Marris and Rein in: Dilemmas of Social Reform (1969). Both of these works offer a sociological analysis which is essential to an understanding of the dynamics of social reform inherent in "citizen participation". They argue that at its roots "citizen participation" is indeed a reform movement, based on a set of assumptions about poverty and how it can be eradicated. These analyses center around the aspects of change with which this reform movement was concerned, and the particular set of strategies employed to achieve its goals. How then did the idea evolve, through what institutions were the strategies operationalized, and what sets of constraints did this reform movement encounter? The following section is a composite sketch of the genealogy of citizen participation as analyzed by these and other students of the subject.

The Idea: Philanthropy and The Intellectual Community Sanction a "New Style of Reform"

During the 1950's, the Ford Foundation became particularly interested in the problems of metropolitan government and urban renewal. In January of 1959, the Foundation allocated its first grants for supporting direct intervention in the social problems of decaying neighborhoods. These grants came as a response to a request by fifteen school superintendents in large cities who were seeking assistance in the development of a forum on the problems of inner city education. Given its concern for the general problem of poverty as a whole, not

just educational achievement, the efforts of the Foundation gradually gave way
to a comprehensive program of action -- called the Gray Areas Projects. These
projects were aimed at demonstrating -- in neighborhoods of five cities, and
one state:

> "...how the city might redeem its broken promise. They
> sought to challenge the conservatism of an impoverished
> school system; open worthwhile careers to young people
> disillusioned by neglect; return public and private
> agencies to a relevant and coherent purpose; and en-
> courage a respect for the rights and dignity of the poor."[6]

These events are historically significant in several respects. First, they mark
the recognition of the problems of poverty as somehow endemic to the mechanics
of the market economy. Moynihan states this recognition this way:

> "...if the economy were to continue to expand, the number
> of persons in the economic difficulties would contract but
> at least not grow. Already a minority, the poor would
> certainly remain one, and very likely become even more so."[7]

Marris and Rein undertook a more detailed examination of the troughs and peaks
of real Gross National Product and noted:

> "Negroes were especially victimized by declining economic
> growth and expanding unemployment, and their plight estab-
> lished the political context from which many of the social
> reforms at the end of the decade [1950's] emerged."[8]

Their examination of this phenomenon caused them to question whether the problems
of minorities were symptomatic of a basic disorder in American society which was
endemic to the market economy.

Second, this phenomenon was recognized by an organization which at this
time in history, and in a country of affluence, had the financial resources necessary to sponsor a program of liberal social reform: The "Gray Area" programs had
as its central thrust an intervening in the urban economic system in order to
create opportunities for those who were victims of the machinations of the market
economy. The projects had therefore been conceived in terms of a strategic cir-
cumvention of the economic phenomena and thus the lack of effectiveness of local
and national policy to deal with the problems of poverty.

Third, the recognition of this phenomenon and the availability of
financial resources invited and sponsored the ideas of professional intellectuals.
It allowed them to apply their skills and insights to the problems of poverty.

The joining of these forces gave impetus to a new idea of social reform. This idea (referred to as a "model" by Moynihan) posited that the forces for change in the system should come from outside the institutions to be changed, i.e., outside the system.

Fourth, the most significant outcome of this chain of events was to be the particular institutional model designed to effect this "liberal social reform movement." As the Ford Foundation graduated from a supporting role to a more direct action involvement in the problems of poverty, it became necessary to create a new agency. It appeared to the Foundation and their technical consultants that the particular limitations of the school system made it an ineffective instrument through which viable solutions of urban poverty could be resolved. Moreover, they envisioned changes in the operation and control of urban institutions as a necessary pre-condition for effective social reform. This new agency, the independent community agency, is referred to by Moynihan as "an invention of enormous power" which in effect proposed a new level of American government.[9]

The Reform Movement is Incorporated and
Sanctioned by the Federal Government

By early 1961, the ideas of the reform movement had been widely diffused. The Mobilization of Youth Program and the Gray Area Projects became a model for President Kennedy's Committee on Juvenile Delinquency program. Both the President's Committee and proponents of the Gray Area Project were convinced that the problems of poverty and juvenile delinquency were strictly related. Both believed that to deal effectively with the problems of poverty, changes should be effected on the system rather than on the symptoms of its dysfunction. In other words, emphasis should be placed upon changing the social environment rather than the individual.[10] The interesting aspect of this notion is that inherent in it is a recognition of a role to be played by the victims of poverty and discrimination. It seemed that the ideas for the solution to the problems of poverty should come from the victims of poverty themselves. To this objective, integration of the "have-nots" inputs to the solution of the problems which plagued them was a crucial aspect of the reform movement. This view recognized that the problems of the poor were not only that they lacked money or will, or that they were "invisible", but that fundamentally they lacked power. As such the "powerlessness" of the "have-not" was seen as the fundamental disorder of the system. Moynihan points out that this recognition emerged as a result of the frustrated attempts by Mobilization for Youth Program (MFY) to implement its program in the urban system. MFY's action programs, then, increasingly became more aware of the "powerlessness" of the poor with respect to city government.[11]

Marris and Rein quote George Brager, executive director of MFY, on this issue:

"Many low income people feel, with justification in fact, a sense of powerlessness. As a result, they have little motivation to learn... The implication for educators is that schools must be prepared to teach minority group members and persons with low incomes the ways in which they can achieve power and use it responsibly to affect their own destinies. Obviously, since the school system itself is a major institution of the society, this means that low-income persons must be taught how to influence the schools as well as other institutions.

The schools do not accept mobilization premise that there is a gap between the system and its low income clientele... The system itself subscribes to the prevailing definition of the low income adult as inadequate and a failure. School officials find it easy to deflect criticism by low-income parents onto the criticizers themselves... It should be no surprise to learn that Mobilization's attempts to bring the schools closer to their lower-class clients have resulted in strongly defensive, near-hysterical resistance.

A further impediment to adequate educational opportunity is the rigidity of the system, its strict hierarchical ordinary and intensive bureaucratic defensiveness."[12]

But the diffusion of the ideas in the "new reform movement" pressed on and found a new audience in the interstices of the federal government. The incorporation of these ideas in the OEO legislation for the Community Action Program completed its ontological cycle. The legislative draft for the "War on Poverty" programs completed the transformation of the social science ideas originally sponsored and operationalized by a private foundation into a sanctioned and legitimized governmental policy. The drafters of the OEO bill were concerned that the "powerlessness" of the poor (specifically southern blacks) might prevent their acquisition of a fair share of the poverty package. As partial insurance against this, the drafters incorporated "maximum feasible participation of the residents of the areas and the members of the groups" involved in the local program. The Community Action Guide of February, 1965, stated the requirement in a language which interpreted "maximum feasible participation" as meaning "the involvement of the poor themselves...in planning, policy making and the operation of the program." The guide suggested that "To be broadly based the Community Action Agency [must include]...the population to be served...." It further suggested that such representatives should be included on the "policy making or governing body of the Community Action Agency" or, where this was not feasible, on a public advisory committee.[13]

The importance of this language is that it placed a strong emphasis on including the "population to be served" on that board which would make policy, rather than on an advisory board. In addition, the CAP guide included another unprecedented feature of resident involvement in federal programs. This was suggested in its language with regard to the permissibility of "protest" activities by "residents, either as individuals, or in groups."[14] Moreover, the guide encouraged "democratic selection procedures which would minimize the possibility that a representative does not command the support or confidence of the group or area that he represents."[15]

Dr. Melvin B. Mogulof noted the significance and precedent-setting nature of these guidelines when he wrote:

"The above provisions in a Federal policy guidebook would be interesting from an academic standpoint, even if they never affected program activity. The fact is that all of these new departures in Federal policy became a living and vital part of many local community action efforts. There is an overwhelming CAP concern with getting representatives of the poor on policy, as opposed to advisory boards; there is a continuing effort to contract with neighborhood groups for program operation; there is a continuing expenditure of Federal resources on community organization which includes the possibility for protest activities; and there is the focus on 'democratizing' the selection procedures for neighborhood representation. Furthermore, all of these activities have entered the stream of Federal Policy thinking, if somewhat erratically."[16]

In sum the drafters of the bill thought it necessary to include the participation requirement based on the following factors:

1. The observation that the workings of the American economy left a segment of the population in a permanent state of poverty.

2. The institutions of the society charged with the amelioration of the symptoms of poverty were considered ineffectual in the discharge of their responsibility.

3. It was recognized, though not universally accepted, that

pressures for change should be directed at the environment (inclusive of its institutions) rather than the victims of poverty themselves.

4. That an important aspect of the system's dysfunction was the "powerlessness" of the poor themselves.

5. A critical factor of any strategy to combat poverty should include the inputs of affected residents in its ultimate formulation.

Summed up, these reasons constitute a comprehensive recognition that the CAP program would be dominated by the (white) political structure.[17] Unless there was some pressure on local urban governments to adopt a different view on the phenomena of poverty, and devise appropriate intervention strategies, its basic causes could not be resolved. It is in this respect that "maximum feasible participation" can be seen as the evolvement of a specific theory of social change.[18]

Systemic Resistance to "Maximum Feasible Participation"

Though the ideas and strategies of the "reform movement" followed a path of transmission through Federal sanction, its practical operationalization in urban localities proved to be more difficult. A number of event herald the resistance that the "reform movement" would encounter. Shortly before the Economic Opportunity Act was signed it was reported in the New York Daily News that the Mobilization for Youth Program had been infiltrated by "commies and commie sympathizers", that funds were being misappropriated and that the program had served as a catalyst to the Harlem riots.[19] At this juncture in the short history of the "reform movement," the fact that the changes were alleged but not proven was overshadowed by the depiction of the program as a potential threat. Shortly after the appearance of these allegations the President's Committee on Juvenile Delinquency program was scrutinized by the now suspicious Congress. Edith Green of the House Committee of Education and Labor reminded the PCJD administrative staff that their mandate was to reduce juvenile delinquency not to reform society.[20]

Similar charges and resistances were also encountered by the Community Action Program. To the extent that MFY presented a threat to urban localities, the CAP program was now considered a potential liability. Mayors from many of the cities where CAP was operationalized protested against the tactics of the Community Action Agencies.

Although the Office of Economic Opportunity only required a one-third representation of the poor (chosen by the residents of the target area) on the Community Action Agency's board, the poor had in a few cases managed to attain majority control of the program. This result angered the chief executives of many cities. Many of them charged that OEO was financing, legitimizing, and training militant activities. Mayor Hugh W. Addonizio told the press after the Newark riots in the summer of 1967:

"The cities were flat on their backs and OEO came along and instead of helping us, as Congress intended, it decided we were a bunch of bullies and it gave the club to the so-called powerless to help beat us as we lay on the ground..."[21]

Mayor Richard J. Daley of Chicago added the weight of a prestigious municipal chief to the protest. He was concerned that the CAP program, which was championing the rights of the poor and accordingly distributing anti-poverty funds, might become a rival to his political machine. While Mayor Daley thought it was appropriate for the program to employ the "poor people of the area," he did not consider their power to allocate funds in the same light. This right should be reserved for him, as Mayor of the city, and as head of the political machine.[22]

With a significant number of municipal chiefs expressing similar sentiments, Mayor Daley led a group of mayors to Washington to have their voice heard. Moynihan reports that after the group met with the President, Johnson emerged persuaded by their arguments and concerns. He quotes the New York Times on November 5, 1965 which stated:[23]

"The Budget Bureau, fiscal arm of the White House, has told the Office of Economic Opportunity that it would prefer less emphasis on policy-making by the poor in planning community projects.

Maximum feasible participation by the poor in the anti-poverty program is called for by the law. In the Bureau's view, this means primarily using the poor to carry out the program, not to design it."

Two years later the mayors' complaints had additional political repercussions in the House of Representatives. The House, responding to the "voice of the people" (represented by the mayors) passed the Green Amendment (bearing the name of Representative Edith Green) as a condition for getting any extension of the Economic Opportunity Act through that governmental body. This amendment gave local governments the option of becoming the Community Action Agency or, designating the private body to act in this capacity. The amendment also dictated that one-third of the seats on CAA governing boards should be occupied by public officials and allowed up to one-third to be occupied by representatives of "business, industry labor, religion, welfare, education, or other major groups of interest in the community."[24] The intent of the Green amendment, of course, was to assure that City Hall would have both hands on the steering wheel of the program's course, thus maintaining the program outside the influence of "militants."

The cumulative effects of these resistances signified a critical halt in the development of the "reform movement". Formerly a significant aspect of the strategy to combat poverty, "maximum feasible participation" was now reduced to a minimum role in the Community Action Program. The sociological analysis of the CAPs efforts led students of the subject to the following conclusions on the failure of the "reform movement":

1. The original theory of "professional reformers" was in error in many respects. It assumed that the poor were unable to respond to opportunity. The operationalization of the program proved this wrong. The poor responded in such great numbers to the opportunities of the Job Core, Head Start, and other OEO programs that it was often impossible to meet their demands.[25]

2. Moreover, the poor, especially ethnic minorities, accepted the analysis of the "system's" shortcomings to effectively deal with poverty. Therefore, whenever and wherever possible they sought to realize "maximum feasible participation." This event militated against the other goals of the program's overall efforts. It both clouded and undermined comprehensiveness and coordination of resources and the rational planning process as integrated goals. In fact, Marris and Rein, conclude that each of these goals is incompatible under the umbrella of a single agency, especially if that agency fosters a philosophy which assumes it knows what is in the best interest of the community. They note:[26]

> "The openness of American society to competing interests and
> new ideas goes with a refusal to allow any preconceived re-
> constitution of a balanced order to forestall further change
> and adoption. Any interested party has the right to propose
> reform - the mayor, a social welfare agency, a redevelopment
> administrator, the poor themselves. None of these is
> obliged to concern himself with the needs of society as a
> whole: he is partisan. Disinterested reformers, whose

concern is not constricted by any jurisdiction, can only influence this 'partisan mutual adjustment' if they too become, in
some sense, partisan - even though their stage in the outcome
is different... It is one thing to create a framework within
which social science can plan coordinated policies: this is a
legitimate and neglected need. But to prescribe how agency
policy is to be reconciled with, say, the demands of Civil
Rights leaders, or how it is to use the insight of social research presupposes the right and wisdom to determine the nature
of society as a whole."

According to these analysts, the cardinal error committed was that
"they tried to establish means, not only to give expression to a variety of
needs, but to determine the way in which these needs should be reconciled. And
this we suggest no one in America has the right to do."[27]

3. The above analysis focuses on the weaknesses of the assumptions
and related planning strategies. Others have viewed the racial conflict associated with the reform movement as the critical factor of its demise. Moynihan
points out for example, that no one (none of the intellectual reformers or their
governmental allies) expected the "powerless" to radically confront the institutions which they deemed unresponsive to their needs. Yet, it should have been
clear that these institutions would/could not accomodate these demands as
rapidly as they were made. Hence the strategy of conflict which promised the
"powerless" effective results, in the long run offered only continued frustration.[28] The frustration of the reformers and the powerless were, of course,
highly related to city and federal officials' resistance to the real and perceived potential threat posed by the reform movement.

The description of this composite history, has concentrated mainly
around the efforts of professional reformers to deal with the phenomena of
poverty in urban America. An attempt has been made to trace the threads which
led to the origins of this movement; the development and sanctioning of the
movement; and finally to resistance, indeed almost a rejection of the notions,
assumptions and strategies inherent in these various intervention efforts.
Yet it could be argued that an important aspect of this genealogy has not been
adequately presented. The sociological analysis thus far presented has not shed
light on the dynamic factors determining the resistance to the "reform movement".
Reference is being made here to the particular dimensions added, but not fully
anticipated, by the "powerless" themselves. For while the "intellectual reformers" sustained a valiant effort to defend "maximum feasible participation"

as a viable solution to poverty, the "powerless" waited unrelieved for real results. They, finally, concluded that "community control" should be their real concern. They had come to realize that although well intentioned, the efforts of the white liberal reformers were at best superficial and ineffective.[29]

But the reform movement was not entirely incompatible with "community control". On the contrary, the reform movement bequeathed to it a philosophy, a certain limited legitimacy, some financial resources and even an organizational base. This philosophy called for the "powerless" to be more self-reliant, to exploit the resources they possessed as a group to combat not only the effects of poverty, but also its corollary: racism. Leonard Fein notes that this development caught the liberal reformers by surprise for it specifically asserted "Blackness", or "Brownness", or "Redness" as identities which the "powerless" could use positively to promote their own cause. In an attempt to trace the factors which contributed to this philosophy he theorizes that black people might have come to this conclusion thusly:

> "Our chief mentors in this battle for civil rights were upper
> middle class liberals, who, for reasons of their own, cling
> to a vision of a universalistic social order. We accepted
> their belief and their doctrine, and acted upon it. It pro-
> duced some rewards, but in the end, we found ourselves still
> unmelted in the hypothetical pot. And, in looking about
> more carefully, we have found that other groups have retained
> their particular identities, have resisted wholesale assimila-
> tion. We conclude, therefore, that liberals are trying to
> impose upon us a standard which derives from their philosophical
> ideal rather than from the sweaty facts of American social life.
> We rather suspect, in fact, that liberals have missed the
> American social experience, for they are in their own way, too
> far removed from its major elements. Moreover, we are inter-
> ested in tactics, not in utopias. We shall, therefore, resist
> being held to a form of behavior which we find both non-
> productive and outside the mainstream of American life, which
> is still in its care, and despite liberal wishes, a group life.
> We shall resist being the guinea pigs for a vision of society
> so out of touch with reality."[30]

To some extent, then, we can presume that the initiative taken by the "powerless" to redefine "maximum feasible participation" in terms of their own reality was also a contributing factor in the resistance encountered by the re-form movement. Probably this episode more than any other in the genealogy of the reform movement brought the debate of the meaning of the phrase "maximum feasible participation" to the fore of national concern. The redefinition of the phrase signaled that in fact the "community control movement" was another of several efforts mounted by blacks and other ethnic minorities to rid themselves of those factors and conditions which have excluded them from their equal share of goods, benefits and status in American society. Thus, the "reform movement" which was promoted by socially conscious professionals, (with an assist from private philanthropy), sanctioned and legitimized by Federal government, coincided with the efforts of "community control" by ethnic minorities. This explains to some degree the need and concern of the mayors and Congress to operationally define the term in a nonthreatening way to local urban systems.

In the following chapter, the Sociology of Knowledge systems theory, will be used to examine the conflicting definitions of "maximum feasible participation". Perhaps through this analysis we can begin to answer why, for example, black people in the urban centers redefined the phrase, and thereby see the implications of this redefinition for the society as a whole.

Footnotes - Chapter I:

1. Austin, David; "Resident Participation, Political Mobilization or Organizational Cooptation?" Findings from the Study of Community Representation in Community Action Agencies, (paper), 1970.

2. Arnstein, Sherri, AIP Journal, p. 216, July, 1969.

3. Model Cities Service Center Bulletin, A Report on Progress (special issue), Vol. 2, No. 9 - 1971, p. 10.

4. Throughout this study the terms "powerless", "have-nots", "residents" and ethnic minorities" are used interchangeably. These terms have been used widely in the literature to categorize those members of society who have fared less than adequately in the acquisition of the total society's goods and services. However, as Melvin Mogulof noted "...the reader should not be confused [by the different terms categorizing the poor]...he must remember that to federal officials of any sophistication, the notion of citizen participation is in part a euphemism for sharing of program authority with the black community." - Citizen Participation: A Review and Commentary on Federal Practices, p. 6.

5. Cahn, Edgar; Passet, Barry; Citizen Participation: Effective Community Change; Praege Publishers, New York, 1971. In the Introduction, the authors build the framework for this reader on citizen participation around this assertion.

6. Marris, Peter; Rein, Martin: Dilemmas of Social Reform; Poverty and Community Action in the United States; Atherton Press, New York, 1969, p. 27.

7. Moynihan, Daniel P.; Maximum Feasible Misunderstanding - Community Action in the War on Poverty; The Free Press, New York, 1969, p. 27.

8. Marris and Rein, op. cit., p. 27.

9. Moynihan, op. cit., p. 13.

10. William Ryans, in his "Blaming the Victim," and several other social scientists have contributed significant analyses of the theoretical and practical implications of this argument.

11. Moynihan, op. cit., p. 111.

12. Marris and Rein, op. cit., p. 111.

13. Community Action Agency Program Guide, Office of Economic Opportunity, February, 1965, p. 1.

14. Ibid., p. 1.

15. Ibid., p. 1.

16. Mogulof, Melvin, <u>Citizen Participation: A Review and Commentary on Policies and Practices</u>, p. 16.

17. Moynihan, <u>op. cit.</u>, p. 87.

18. Moynihan, <u>op. cit.</u>, p. 87.

19. Moynihan, <u>op. cit.</u>, p. 104. Also Marris and Rein, <u>op. cit.</u>, pp. 178-179.

20. Moynihan, <u>op. cit.</u>, p. 76.

21. Sundquist, James, <u>Making Federalism Work, A Study of Program Coordination at the Community Level</u>, The Brookings Institution, 1970, p. 80.

22. Moynihan, <u>op. cit.</u>, p. 80.

23. Moynihan, <u>op. cit.</u>, p. 145.

24. Sundquist, <u>op. cit.</u>, p. 85.

25. Marris and Rein, <u>op. cit.</u>, p. 225.

26. Marris and Rein, <u>op. cit.</u>, p. 227-228.

27. <u>Ibid.</u>, p. 229.

28. Moynihan, <u>op. cit.</u>, p. 143.

29. Fein, Leonard J., <u>The Ecology of the Public Schools, An Inquiry into Community Control</u>, p. 19.

30. Fein, <u>op. cit.</u>, p. 29.

CHAPTER II

SOCIOLOGY OF KNOWLEDGE -- AS AN ANALYTICAL FRAMEWORK

It is clear that the professional intellectual reformers saw a need
for a change in the present institutional order, i.e., the American social system. Many of the frustrations that resulted from the experiences of the Gray
Areas, PCJD, MFY and CAA programs made it even clearer to black and other ethnic
minorities that the system's response to these efforts to change the institutional
order was increased social control. The system remained opposed to changing the
institutional order to include black people and other ethnic minority groups as
legitimate participants. To date there have been several sociological inquiries
which have noted a pattern of increased social control in the systemic reactions
to the community control issues. This pattern could be considered as a form of
institutional cooptation whereby the "powerless" are invited to become involved
administratively but not substantively in making those decisions that affect
their very lives. It is in this light that the reaction of the city mayors and
eventually Congress will be considered. It will also be suggested that the most
dynamic area of conflict occurs over which operational definition of "resident
participation" will prevail, and that this conflict is a manifestation of black
peoples' and white peoples' socio-historical relationship.

Like every slave rebellion or revolt, the redefinition of "resident
participation" sought to change the relationship and the "socio-political-
economic" factors that have characterized the relationship between these groups
of people. This relationship has been appropriately described by Winthrop Jordan
in his national best seller White over Black.[1] To a considerable extent, this
relationship has defined the structural processes and conditions through which
these groups interact with each other.

It is beyond the scope of this study to attempt an epistemological
analysis of this relationship. But some attempt, albeit a limited one, will be
made at a contextual understanding of this relationship.

It is an historical perhaps more importantly an "existential fact"
(constantly affirmed existence in time and space), that black people did not
voluntarily migrate to the Americas. They were uprooted from their homelands,
enslaved, and brought to this country to serve the economic (among others?)
interests of white Europeans. This is the "existential fact" that both white

and black people have had to live with - bounded as they are with the same society. This is the "existential fact" that white people justified and rationalized, using every resource that they commanded inclusive of their culture, religion, tradition and schools (instruments of the socializing process). W. E. B. DuBois, a social theorist, examined the consequences of slavery for black people and noted:

> "Labor was degraded, humanity was despised, the theory of 'race' arose. There came a new doctrine of universal labor: mankind were of two sorts -- the superior and the inferior; the inferior toiled for the superior and the superior were real men, the inferior half men or less. Among the white lords of creation there were 'lower classes' resembling the inferior darker folks. Where possible, they were to be raised to equality with the master class. But no equality was possible or desirable for 'darkies'. In line with this conviction, the Christian Church, Catholic and Protestant, at first damned the heathen blacks with the 'curse of Canaan', then held out hope of freedom through 'conversion' and finally acquiesced in a <u>permanent</u> status of human slavery."[2] (emphasis added)

DuBois goes on to say:

> "In addition to this, it went without saying that the people of Europe had a right to live upon the labor and the property of the colored people of the World. In order to establish the righteousness of this point of view, science and religion, government and industry, were wheeled into line. The word 'Negro' was used for the first time in the world's history to tie color to race and blackness to slavery and degradation. The white race was pictured as 'pure' and superior; the black as dirty, stupid, and inevitably inferior; the yellow race as sharing, in deception and cowardice, much of this color inferiority; white mixture of races was considered the prime cause of degradation and failure in civilization. Everything great, everything fine, everything successful in human culture, was white.[3]

DeBois' analysis places the issue squarely within the historical context and views the rationalization of the "existential fact" as the conditioning factor of the relationship between the two groups.

Those social scientists who purport to engage in value-free inquiries offer us an analytical framework which, although it does not take into primary consideration the "existential fact", is considerably useful to our analysis. The social system theory sees everyone interacting in a social system with limited flexibility. To the extent that flexibility within the system is limited, strain or conflict, will inevitably develop. Conflict (or strain) is handled by ordering groups within the system according to either inferior or superior status. The distribution of goods and services, prestige and status are allocated and distributed in accordance with the customs and traditions of society. (Keeping in mind, of course, that this arrangement best serves the group who holds the power -- the power to design the relationships in the first place.) This theory further holds that any change in the basic arrangement would result in chain-reaction throughout the entire system causing its destruction.[4]

This structural analysis depicts the system's basic configuration as being inflexible to change. It is implicitly assumed that the relationship of the groups (inferior and superior) necessarily must remain constant if the system is to remain intact. Any challenge to the existing order is a threat to the very survival of society itself. Hence the need to control any group that poses either a theoretical or practical threat to the existing institutional order.

At this point, we will turn to the sociology of knowledge as a framework which encompasses both analytical frameworks presented above, i.e., the historical framework and the social system framework.

Berger and Luckman's book, The Social Construction of Reality - a Treatise in the Sociology of Knowledge has as a basic premise that there is no objective, independent "reality". They assume, rather, that "reality" is a social construction of people bounded basically by a common interest. Necessary for their co-existence is a consensus about their environment and how to deal with it in a manner around which they can interact with a minimum of conflict. Consensus is arrived at by way of reconciliatory agreements among the individuals within the group. Final agreements result in social institutions which begin the process of "objectifying reality". This later stage in the development of "reality" serves the greater function of providing structured regularity and continuity for succeeding generations. "Objective reality", socially developed, becomes legitimized in order for the social system of the group to continue. Conceptual machinery, i. e., instruments of social control, is developed for the implicit purpose of socializing members within the group. Socialization becomes the process by which the group transmits "objective reality". Young members of the group are socialized, and thus, gain "knowledge". This "knowledge", socially constructed, legitimized and objectified, finally becomes seen as "reality" or "truth", thus completing the ontological cycle.[5]

The thesis of the book is that "reality" is socially defined and has to be defended against any other version of "reality" similarly defined. Therefore, what "knowledge" is promoted and enforced becomes positively correlated to power:

> "Specifically, the success of particular conceptual machineries is related to the power possessed by those who operate them. The confrontation of alternative symbolic universes implies a problem of power - which of the conflicting definitions of reality will be 'made to stick' in the society. Two societies confronting each other with conflicting universes will both develop conceptual machineries designed to maintain their respective universes....Which if the two will win, however, will depend more on the power than on the theoretical ingenuity of the respective legitimators."[6]

As regards the issues raised by "community control", several areas of conflict emerged. Among them were the issues of "community", racial identity, and the questions of political power. These three areas are intimately related. Several critics have noted the factors which created the mood, or more specifically, the initiatives on part of the powerless to create an "alternative reality". The Civil Rights Movement, for example, was strongly allied with the efforts of the professional reformers in the Gray area, and PCJD programs. The Civil Rights Movement,[7] however, tended to accept on faith the importance of integration as a desirable goal. This emphasis, associated with a strategy of moral appeal, led to a de-emphasis on the social heritage and the creative potential of the black community. Based on these observations, Fein noted:

> "In effect, the liberal community, both black and white, was caught up in a wrenching dilemma. The only way, it appeared, to move a sluggish nation towards massive amelioration of the Negro condition was to show how terrifyingly debilitating were the effects of discrimination and bigotry. The more lurid the details, the more guilt it would evoke, and the more guilt, the more readiness to act. Yet the same lurid detail that did, in the event, prompt large-scale federal programs, also reinforced white convictions that Negroes were undesirable objects of interaction."[8]

If the emphasis on integration and its associated strategies had partial negative effects on the white community, its effects (coupled by the overall failure of the movement) were equally significant for the black community. The resistance of the city mayors and Congress exacerbated the contradictions of integration as a goal.[9] As Malcolm X pointed out, it is not a matter of integration versus separation, the issue is rather human liberation.[10] Thus to the extent that the efforts of the "reform movement" promised results at the cost of self-affirmation (racial identification) it was rejected by black people themselves. This rejection propelled a momentum among black people in many regions across the country which led to an affirmation of an "alternative reality". The momentum was characterized by their espousal of a wave of alternative concepts enfolded in the banner of black power. They then began to redefine themselves in terms of their racial identity, their blackness:

> "Blackness is a political/cultural concept. It recognizes
> man's need for a knowledge of where he has been in order
> to determine where he must go. It affirms an identity
> that is African in root, understanding that an infusion of
> European and Asiatic strains has possibly expanded but cer-
> tainly not destroyed that basic African identity.
>
> Blackness is a political/cultural concept powered by the
> demands of Man's moral and spiritual nature. It emphasized
> the indivisibility of Man with the One Force, securing
> therefore forever the dignity of the individual and his
> right to freedom by whatever means necessary.
>
> Blackness is a political/cultural concept called "revolution-
> ary" by the oppressor because it identified the oppressor,
> defines the nature of his oppresionistic acts and frees the
> mind of the oppressed.
>
> Blackness is the political/cultural concept that actuates
> the man who has determined to direct his own destiny, formu-
> late his own definitions, construct his own guidelines and
> forge his own values. It understands that American democracy
> has been from the beginning a fascist system based on racism
> and that the issue from the beginning and now, is control.
> It advocates Black control in the degree necessary to serve
> the best interest of Blacks and with the realization that old
> governmental systems do not serve the best interest of Blacks.
> It understands that freedom by any means necessary is the
> only acceptable alternative to bondage by whatever name.
>
> Blackness is a political/cultural concept which calls the
> individual to view the nobility of his ancestral civiliza-
> tions, the tragedy of his slave/castration involvement with
> America, and the magnificance of his courage under oppressive
> odds, with the understanding that this is where he has been.
> Where he goes now becomes his major consideration, and how he
> must go, his most pressing business.
>
> Blackness is a political/cultural concept that is innovative.

It endorses a creative Family-Nation which dismisses an alien tradition and re-thinks forms, systems and methodologies - placing Black minds, Black energies, and Black resources to a common goal; the creation of a New Man, and a re-directed, re-shaped Society supportive of him."[11]

This marks the beginning of what James Turner calls "the process of Black re-socialization." New norms and role models for social performance and cultural attitudes begin to be formed. Black people began differentiating themselves further within the social system as having a different/characteristic history, a different "place" in the institutional order, a different/characteristic set of values, than white members of the American society.[12]

This process can be identified within the framework of the sociology of knowledge as the stage where a group of people bounded in common interest (Black people) begins to build a consensus about their environment (American society). As has been previously noted, black people and other ethnic minorities attempted to operationalize the cultural and political values of this consensus in the social institutions created by the "reform movement" (MFY and CAA community agencies). The essential purpose of using the resources of these agencies, (following the logic of the sociology of knowledge), was to begin a process of "objectifying reality". In this way, it was hoped, the "process of Black re-socialization" would provide structured regularity and continuity for succeeding Black generations. To the extent that they succeeded, the community action agencies (theoretically and practically), became a "conceptual machinery", i.e., an instrument of social control - with the potential to transmit an "alternative objective reality".

Politically, a black social scientist describes this "alternative objective reality" as the essence of black nationalism:

"The essential theme of black nationalism can be seen as a counter-movement away from subordination to independence, from alienation through repudiation to self-affirmation. In this respect such a movement of ideas represents an effort to transcend the immediate condition of an undesirable relationship by a process of reflection which creates a different (and opposing) constellation of symbols and assumptions. Black nationalism is thus at once a movement of both socio-psychological and political portent."[13]

Theoretically, the creation of an "alternative objective reality" leads the black nationalist to see self-definition and self-determination as concomittant. He or she then predicates a new "self-perception" upon terms that are non-normative or divergent from white-western values. It is the belief of the black nationalist that only by promoting this "alternative objective reality" will it be possible to develop a sense of a Black Community.[14] This, in turn, should create a condition where effective change can be promoted in the social system. Such change would address itself to:

1. The questioning of old values and institutions of the society;

2. The searching for new and different forms of political structures to solve socio-economic problems;

3. The broadening of the base of political participation in the social system to include more people in the decision making process.

Change, of course, is directed toward the institutional order. By promoting a redefinition of "participation" which, in substance, reflected the philosophy of Black nationalism, the "powerless" threatened the ability of the institutional order to define "reality" to its inhabitants. Berger and Luckman noted:

> "The group that has objectivated this deviant reality becomes the carrier of an alternative definition of reality. It is hardly necessary to belabor the point that such heretical groups posit not only a theoretical threat to the symbolic universe but a practical one to the institutional order legitimized by the symbolic universe in question. The repressive procedures customarily employed against such groups by the custodians of the 'official' definition of reality need not concern us in this context. What is important for us to consider is the need for such repression to be legitimized, which, of course, implies the setting in motion of various concepted machineries designed to maintain the 'official' universe against the heretical universe."[15] (emphasis added)

Thus, as some writers and spokespeople for the community action agencies increasingly emphasized, the "powerlessness" of the poor with respect to city government and devised strategies accordingly, they posed a challenge to that very government. That challenge was met by the city mayors with the assistance of Congress. As previously noted, the Executive Office of the President kept the role of the poor in policy-making to a minimum.

The social system, then, remained within the constraints imposed by the Green amendments in what William Gamson refers to as a condition of "stable unrepresentation."[16] Gamson analyzes the American political system as operatively structured in a manner which prevents "incipient competitors" from gaining entry into the political system. Necessarily, such groups must resort to norm violating behavior if they are to win entry into the political system. He classifies these groups as "unrepresented groups". They are characterized by not having any influence with authorities or influential interest groups within the political system through which their interest can be promoted. Given these conditions a state of stable unrepresentation exists, whereby the system functions to:

> "Keep unrepresented groups from developing solidarity and political organizing and to discourage their effective entry into the competitive establishment if and as they become organized. The competitive establishment is boundary-maintaining process involves various kinds of social control."[17]

Gamson's "stable unrepresentation" model, lends itself to the present analysis. For example, it could be argued that the "powerless" by definition constitute an "unrepresented" group. Moreover, to the extent that they attempted to promote their redefinition of participation through the existing system, they got no positive response. Moynihan, in fact, states that those community action agencies which were closely controlled by City Hall were ineffective, and those which were seen to be antagonistic were destroyed.[18] The study by David Austin on resident participation in the CAP details similar conclusions. In regard to official federal policy on resident participation to the patterns of participation actually found in local CAA's - he concluded:[19]

1. Community Action Agencies did not instutionalize, as an ongoing operational process, a broadly decentralized process of citizen participation in organizational decision making.

2. The agency did not create participatory democracy around significant decision making or establish popular sovereignty over the operation of a set of service programs.

3. To a substantial degree, the structure of participation and the operation of participation was built around a model of advisory and co-opted participation within the operating constraints of a rather traditional model of the non-governmental social welfare service agency.

These conclusions appear to have a degree of predictability within Gamson's theoretical model, i.e., the institutional system is structured in such a way that it discouraged the translation of grievances into political demands which can be effectively pursued through systemic political action.

Summary Conclusions

The theoretical models outlined in this section highlight the characteristics of the "heretic/deviant" groups and the normal institutional response to challenge forwarded by any such group. The Berger-Luckman model, though, adds a pertinent characteristic that is not underscored by the others, namely the need for the response to be legitimized. They refer to legitimization as the process of "explaining" and justifying the institutional order. It is therefore not only necessary to repress the existing threat to the institutional order, but to justify that repression as well. As long as there is no existing threat (actual or potential), the institutional order (symbolic universe) is self-maintaining, i.e., self-legitimizing. Therefore, when the "symbolic universe" has a problem, specific "universe-maintenance" procedures are set in motion. Specific "conceptual machineries" are maintained for this purpose.

Evidence of the conceptual machinery in action is reflected in the aforementioned reports in the New York Times identifying Community Action Agencies as havens for communist infiltrators. In addition, several well-known "scholars" have questioned the validity of the existence of a "Black culture" much less a "Black community". They argue that black people in America have no history or culture to defend -- that they are in essence true Americans.[20] More recently there have been several "scientific" efforts aimed at identifying the genetic difference between blacks and whites. The findings of these efforts to date seem to support the notion that black people are not as well endowed (genetically) as white people.[21] These claims are made in addition to those of some policy makers that:

1. The Government cannot subsidize "revolution."

2. The poor do not know what is good for them, otherwise they would not be poor.

3. What the poor need are jobs, not organizing into troublemaking groups.

4. Citizen participation only stirs controversy, causes delays and polarizes the differences between races and classes.

5. Citizen participation bent on community control is inimical to governmental honesty, equity and professionalism.

6. Citizen participation places undue constraints on the capacity of local government to act on decisions based on city-wide rather than more

parochial considerations.[22]

These claims further serve to maintain the symbolic universe from attack. The systemic view emerges: in "reality" there are no basic problems in the institutional order, but rather such problems as they do exist are with the "heretics/deviants". Practically they represent a conceptual machinery which aims at the elimination of any other interpretation of reality that does not fit into the symbolic universe. The "norm-violators" are first given a negative ontological status. Second, they are explained away in terms of concepts belonging to the institutional order's perception of what is "real": As Berger and Luckman put it:

> "The deviant conceptions are not merely assigned a negative status, they are grappled with theoretically in detail. The final goal of the procedure is to incorporate the deviant conceptions within one's own universe. In this manner, the negation of one's universe is subtly changed into an affirmation of it. The presupposition is always that the negator does not really know what he is saying. His statements become meaningful only as they are translated into more 'correct' terms, that is, terms deriving from the universe he negates."[23]

The theoretical models presented here, then, underscore the importance of power. Power is sought by black people through a recognition of their collective identity; power is sought by black people for self-determination. The critical area of focus is the power to define the situation, the power to maintain the "symbolic universe," the power to produce "reality" and the power to ward off challenges to an heretical view of the symbolic universe's reality. The apparent response of municipal governments and official policy makers to neutralize black people's "alternative reality" by assigning it to an inferior ontological status is to alleviate conflict without surrendering authority (or power) -- without changing the relationship between the black people and the dominant culture. This process, of course, does not incorporate the basic issues most minority groups are raising. Furthermore, social change of the kind demanded by ethnic minorities is not likely to be realized within the "modus operandi", structured by the traditional definition of reality. That it was necessary to set in motion conceptual machineries to maintain and reaffirm the reality of the present institutional order may prolong and exacerbate severe conflict instead of preventing it. Does this process reflect the institutional order's inability to recognize the problems of the poor -- specifically the ethnic poor? Or does it, in fact, reflect its unwillingness? These are

31

questions that must be answered, because the problem seems to be the traditional definition of reality itself -- a "reality" which inhibits social change. What is needed is a restructuring of "reality" if real social changes of the sort ethnic minority groups now demand are to be realized. Significantly, the development of citizen participation as it has evolved through its several phases does offer a potential mechanism for such a restructuring. John Friedman argues this point in a cogent article entitled "The Public Interest and Community Participation: Toward a Reconstruction of Public Philosophy."[24] His argument supports the legitimacy of the claims promoted by the "powerless" that the American system of government is structured in such a manner that it produces results that are often unjust. The outcome of such a system, then, does not ultimately serve the general public interest. On this basis, he argues, what is needed is the identification and commitment to a "moral good" to guide the governance of the American society. This implies the identification of an equitable and legitimate process in the allocation and uses of power. The operationalization of this process, however, would mean at a minimum:

> "...a redistribution of power from those who now enjoy a
> surplus to those who now do not have enough. The questions
> of power turns out to be the crucial one. People require
> effective power to control their immediate environment in
> order to make it more agreeable to their lives. They also
> require influence, or power, to shape the larger environ-
> ments - physical, economic, cultural and political - which
> impinge on their lives in a multiplicity of ways."[25]

Citizen participation could be a mechanism through which an equitable and legitimate distribution of the cumulative goods and services of society is realized. But participation has to be defined and operationalized in such a manner that a redistribution of power can be affected:

> "...to participate means not only gaining a voice in and
> having a measure of influence over the allocation and uses
> but also in the sharing the patrimony or the wealth of the
> community and thus in the outcomes of the established sys-
> tems of governance. In this manner our discussion of the
> public good is directly related to considerations concerning
> the processes and substance of community participation."[26]

To a large extent, then, "citizen participation" is a recognition that the weakness of the redistribution mechanism in American society is a crucial cause of poverty. Ethnic minority groups have shared less than equally in the basic rewards of American society. The participation of the "powerless" in the planning, operation and development of the program was provided as an assurance that resources would be allocated to meet the needs of the poor as they saw them. However, the concept and the requirement have been met with resistance; in essence we could say that there has been a conflict between the "system's" definition and that of the "have-nots". The question becomes, then, to what extent can the government or "the guardians of the system" both sponsor and control citizen participation without undermining the assurance that resources will be allocated to meet the "have-nots" needs as they see these needs. Roland Warren reformulated this question concisely when he asked:

> "Can the system right what an increasing number of people are becoming to consider to be its tragic wrongs -- both at home and abroad -- before it disintegrates under the im- mobilization? under the twin pressures of external rebellion and internal axomix immobilization? or will it be destroyed? Or do we confront the prospect of still another century of exploitation and racial prejudice?"[27]

The Model Cities program is the most recent national intervention program which has incorporated "citizen participation". As such the program provides an appropriate arena to examine in more detail the dynamics of "citizen participation": How is it defined operationally? Is it meeting the needs of the poor? How significant is its potential as a mechanism through which the powerless can increase their influence in those decisions which affect their lives? Is the participation process as evolved to date in the Model Cities program effective? And, if so, under what conditions?

Footnotes - Chapter II:

1. Winthrop Jordan in his book White over Black traces the historical and sociological factors which contributed to racial prejudice.

2. DuBois, W. E. B., The World and Africa, International Co., Inc., New York, p. 19.

3. DuBois, op. cit., p. 19.

4. Gordon, W. Allport, The Nature of Prejudice, Doubleday and Company, Inc., 196 , New York; pp. 465-467.

5. Berger, Peter L. and Luckman, Thomas, The Social Construction of Reality: A Treatise on the Sociology of Knowledge; Doubleday and Company, Inc., Garden City, New York, Chapter II.

6. Berger and Luckman, op. cit., p. 108-109.

7. Several critics - Kenneth Clark among them - make this point about the Civil Rights Movement. It is seen as a movement rooted in the "universal brotherhood of man". As such, it pursues the normative goals of social Christianity. Clark argues, for example, that the Civil Rights Movement has its own historic and impersonal momentum, responsive to deep and powerful economic, and international events and political and ideological forces beyond the control of individuals, agencies or government. "The Civil Rights Movement," Daedalus, Winter-Spring, 1966.

8. Fein, op. cit., p. 6.

9. Integration is taken to mean here the acceptance of black people into the mainstream of American society on their individual merits, without regard to their color, race or creed.

10. Malcolm X, Malcolm X Speaks, "The Message to the Grass Roots," New York, Grove Press, 1965.

11. Mari, Evans, "Definition of Blackness," Negro Digest, November, 1969, pp. 34-35. Although there has been many, and varying definitions of "Blackness" - this one can be considered as one of the more integrated, comprehensive - and poetic.

12. Turner, James, "The Sociology of Black Nationalism," article in The Black Scholar, December, 1969, p. 18.

13. Turner, op. cit., p. 18.

14. Stokely Carmichael and Charles Hamilton, Black Power - The Politics of Liberation in America, Bantage Books, New York, 1967, p. 39.

15. Berger and Luckman, op. cit., p. 107.

15. Berger and Luckman, op. cit., p. 107.

16. Gamson, William, "Stable Unrepresentation in American Society" - article in American Behavioral Scientist.

17. Gamson, op. cit., p.

18. Moynihan, op. cit., p. 130.

19. Austin, Public Administration review - Special issue, September, 1972, Vol. XXXII, p. 419.

20. Norman Glazer and Patrick Moynihan, Beyond the Melting Pot, MIT Press, Cambridge, Massachusetts, 1963.

21. Jensen, Arthur, "How Much Can We Boost IQ and Scholastic Achievement?", Environment, Heredity, and Intelligence, Harvard Educational Review, Reprint Series No. 2, 1969, p. 1-125.

22. Cahn, Edgar, Passet, Barry, editors: Citizen Participation: Effective Community Change, Praeger Special Studies in U.S. Economic and Social Development, New York, p. 14.

23. Berger and Luckman, op. cit., p. 16.

24. Friedman, John, in "Journal of the American Institute of Planners," January, 1973, Vol. 39, #1.

25. Friedman, John, article in Journal of Social Planning, January 1, 1973, p. 6.

26. Ibid., p. 7.

27. Warren, Roland; (Editor), Politics and the Ghettoes, Atherton Press, New York, 1969, p. 29.

CHAPTER III

THE MODEL CITIES PROGRAM AND THE ISSUES OF RESIDENT PARTICIPATION

Enacted in 1966, The Model Cities program, is a federal government intervention effort dealing with the myriad social and economic problems of the urban poor. The program is intended to increase the capabilities of some 150 cities to deal effectively with poverty and its effects on the deterioration of residential neighborhoods and on the individuals who are caught in its tentacles.

In 1965, prior to the creation of the Department of Housing and Urban Development, President Johnson assembled a task force on urban problems. The group was headed by Robert Wood of MIT and later became known as the Wood Task Force. One of its most pressing concerns was to develop viable processes through which urban renewal and social programs could be planned in a coordinated manner to meet the dual objectives of the ghetto residents and the city planners.[1] And it is out of the efforts of this task force that the basic assumptions, strategies and ideas that later would underlie the Model Cities Program originated.

Professor Judson James of the City University of New York has outlined a brief history of the Wood Task Force. He wrote:

> "The task force was selected with an eye to avoiding people committed to existing programs and was given a charge to develop new and innovative programs. Later, responsibility was added for a re-organization of HUD......Substantial agreement was reached early that mayors and city councils were to have a principal role; that physical and social planning should be coordinated; and that racial integration and citizen participation were desirable goals but would have to be played down in order to facilitate congressional passage."[2]

It was Professor James' contention that the most important justification of the Model Cities program was to implement a new intervention effort in the "slums of American cities" and to tackle the problem of coordination of intergovernmental relations.[3] Closely linked to the latter was a second major concern, formulated by HUD's assistant secretary, H. Ralph Taylor, in his explanation of Model Cities as a

> "demonstration designed to experiment with and test solutions and the will and competence of communities to meet the problems of slums."[4]

These two major emphases, coordination and the provision of adequate services to ameliorate the deteriorating conditions of the slums, constituted the cornerstone of the Program. It was assumed that because of the overlapping, inconsistent, uncoordinated manner through which federal money flowed into localities, a series of irrational constraints had impeded success in arresting the plight of the urban poor and their physical surroundings. The solution to this problem, then, was sought through some means of rational planning and the development of coordinating mechanisms which could rid the cities of the many problems with which they were faced.

Given this important charge and offering a seemingly viable procedure toward arresting the plight of the cities, the Model Cities legislation had a hard path to carve out before its congressional passage. Robert B. Semple, Jr., writing in the New York Times of November 4, 1966, depicts the rocky stages through which the Model Cities legislation passed. He summarizes those several states this way:

> "'The Demonstration Cities Act had many crises on its way to
> passage. Anticipatory revisions by the Wood Task Force were
> proven justifiable by the narrow margins of passage. Even
> with the considerable legislative contribution of Senator
> Muskie of Maine; further downplaying of citizen participation
> and racial integration was necessary. The basic provisions
> of the legislation survived, but the supplemental funding
> authorization was cut from 5 years to 2, and additional housing
> and renewal funds were added to sweeten the passage.' The
> Editor of this piece noted: The Final version of the bill
> also knocked out the 'federal coordinators' which HUD had
> sought to assist each city in pulling together federal funds
> and programs; removed a policy declaration that housing pro-
> grams under the act should have elimination of racial segrega-
> tion as an objective; and bussing of children into integrated
> schools as a condition of assistance."[5]

Thus, from its beginnings the Model Cities Program was marked by con-servatism, especially in regards to areas of race relations, and definitely vis-a-vis its provision for "widespread citizen participation." Indeed, one could infer from the various crises, "cutbacks", and "cutoffs" of the original Model Cities Legislation and its final emphasis on the role of the city, that the Model Cities Legislation was a reaction to the style and degree of resident involvement in the Community Action Program effort.[6]

The Program was passed by Congress with the appropriate and necessary deletions in November, 1966. Its basic objectives, as originally intended by the Wood Task Force, remained coordination and concentration of Federal, State, and local resources development of innovative approaches to "improve the quality of life' in the Model Neighborhoods; and "meaningful citizen participation" in the planning and development process. Guidelines from the Department of Housing and Urban Planning (HUD), the administering agency, laid out a rational, orderly, sequential planning process:

1. Identification and analysis of Model Neighborhoods major problems and especially their causes and the interrelationships of their causes; definition of long range goals; programs to achieve these goals, and priorities and strategies for implementation.

2. Quantification of five-year objectives and cost for the Model Neighborhood plan as the framework for first year action programs. The five year plans and first year operating plans covered housing, education, transportation, employment, social services, crime prevention and control, etc. Once the plans were completed, the Model Cities agencies had to prepare separate applications for federal funds from each federal agency.

The Department of Housing and Urban Development invited cities to enter competition for a place in the program. The program has now gone through two rounds of city selection, during each of which seventy-five cities were chosen. Although "any municipality, county or other public body having general governmental powers was eligible to apply for assistance under the program,"[7] the great majority of participating units are cities.

Administration of the Program

One of the most ambitious and challenging aspects of the Program is its mandate to concentrate under the umbrella of the CDA all relevant federal, state, local and private resources. The crux of the challenge lies in the problem of bringing together several groups of actors who not only have never worked together before but have in fact been previously hostile toward each other. Elected officials, public and private agencies, and neighborhood residents each have a role.

The HUD office in Washington has general policy and administrative responsibility for the Model Cities program. Staff members in this office are responsible for maintaining liaison with each of the Regional Offices and for coordinating the evaluation submissions from and technical assistance to participating localities in each of the Regions.

One of the principal stated aims of the Model Cities Program is to make local governments more responsible and responsive to the needs of low income residents. This stated responsibility involved developing the competence of local agencies to analyze problems, commit resources, and implement programs which would effectively deal with poverty and its effects in the Model Neighborhoods. The program has decided that the most effective way to achieve these aims is by emphasizing the authority of local government, i.e., City Hall. CDA Letter #10 states that:

> The City Executive Officer and the local governing body shall assume early, continuous, and ultimate responsibility for the development, implementation, and performance of the Model Cities Program. (p. 2)

This determined effort to underline the authority and ultimate responsibility of the program within the confines of city government was to insure stability in the intervention process. It reflects the concern of the Model Cities Program authors that the City Demonstration Agencies should recognize that their allegiance must be to City Hall rather than to the target neighborhood residents. The reasoning behind this concern, of course, was to guarantee that the essential coordinating function of the program would not be lost.[8]

Section 112(2) of the Model Cities statute defines the "City Demonstration Agency" as:

> "The City, the county, or any local public agency established or designated by the local governing body of such city or county to administer the comprehensive city demonstration program."

A further description of the CDA contained in the Program Guide, Chapter I, paragraph 1.3.1, requires that where the city or county itself is the CDA, responsibility for the program management must be in "a single administrative unit that can draw on the powers of the chief executive." If a local public agency is to be designated, the Program Guide requires that it be one closely related to the chief executive officer, endowed with broad powers, and adequately staffed. HUD has stipulated that the CDA may contract for assistance in the planning and implementation of the program, but it cannot delegate total responsibility for the program to a non-profit corporation.[9] Although some residents may work out a relationship with the CDA whereby they have "vetoes" over the program content, Assistant Secretary Hyde states that the CDA must "retain the ability to move the program."[10]

As can be discerned, then, the authors and early administrators of the Model Cities program were conservative in the administrative structuring of the Model Cities program. This character of administrative conservatism was widespread and insured not only City Hall's dominance in the program but also in the intervention process: maximizing existing resources, rehabilitating existing structures, preserving existing neighborhoods, and, of course, using existing political institutions to deal with the problems of poverty. In essence, the idea from whence the program was developed was conservative; the authors were more concerned with practicality than with ideology.

This streak of conservatism can perhaps be explained as a reaction to two circumstances, one historical and the other procedural. The 1960's witnessed an explosion of the latent hostilities of ghetto dwellers throughout urban America. By the end of 1966, Model Cities was promulgated and designed as a solution -- not as a cause (like urban renewal) of urban unrest. The authors of the program were probably concerned that the intervention process should insure stability and orderly change in dealing with the problems of poverty. To do this they had to learn from experience, in this case, the experience of the Community Action Program. From this perspective, one could indeed say that the Model Cities program was structured to incorporate the negative experiences of the CAP. But the CAP had set a precedent and became an aid to a growing momentum within the ghettos of America that would be difficult to halt, despite the "Green Amendments."

Survey of Issues in Resident Participation

Earlier we noted the structural and procedural differences between "maximum feasible participation" and "widespread citizen participation." Yet there remains considerable question, on the part of residents and chief executive of how different "participation" would be under the Model Cities Program. The Department of Housing and Urban Development has responded by requiring that the city involve model neighborhood area residents in the program "in a meaningful way." No precise formula for resident participation has been promulgated, and the implementation of the requirement has been left up to the cities themselves.

The Model Cities version of "widespread citizen participation repre-sents a retreat from the OEO brand of "maximum feasible participation."

Community action agencies of the OEO poverty program were more independent of City Hall, and prior to the Green Amendment offered far more flexibility as regards resident participation. We have seen that the Model Cities program is placed under the close supervision of the chief executive's office; all Model Cities grants must be made to the CDA, a public agency established or designated by the city. Although "widespread citizen participation" is required (Section 103[a] of the Demonstration Cities and Metropolitan Act of 1966), the local governing body must approve the Model Cities Program and the application for assistance. These were not the requirements for the CAAs.

Nonetheless, the goal of resident participation in Model Cities has retained the basic outlines originally set forth under the Gray areas and CAP programs. Among the major assumptions are:

... acknowledging the basic social right of people affected by public programs to have access to and influence on the process by which decisions about their lives are made.

... accepting the fact that even the best intentioned officials and technicians are often, by their training, experience, and life-styles, unfamiliar with or even insensitive to the problems and aspirations of Model Neighborhood residents; therefore, resident input will result in more relevant, sensitive, and effective plans.

... recognizing that the process of participation makes it possible for those formerly excluded from the system to learn how to make it function in their interest.

... confronting the reality that generations of exploitation, or what has been perceived as exploitation, has created considerable distrust of public officials among poor people; guaranteeing neighborhood residents technical assistance in planning thereby insuring their trust in that planning.[11]

Although this list does not exhaust the objectives of citizen participation in Model Cities, it makes clear the fact that the overall "public good," as demonstrated by the quality of life in American cities, cannot be improved unless all citizens, especially ethnic minority groups and public officials, develop processes and mechanisms at all levels of government, for assessing problems, developing strategies and planning programs together.

HUD has given the cities primary responsibility for defining the specific form "widespread citizen participation" should take. There are, however, a series of minimal "performance standards":

> "In order to provide the citizen participation called for in the Act, there must be some form of organizational structure, existing or newly established, which involves neighborhood residents in the process of policy and program implementation and operation. The leadership of that structure must consist of persons whom neighborhood residents accept as representing their interest.
>
> The neighborhood citizen structure must have clear and direct access to the decision-making process of the City Demonstration Agency so that neighborhood views can influence policy, planning and program decisions. That structure must have sufficient information about any matter to be decided for a sufficient period of time so that it can initiate proposals and react knowledgeably to proposals from others. In order to initiate and react intelligently in program matters, the structure must have the technical capacity for making knowledgeable decisions. This will mean that some form of professional technical assistance, in a manner agreed to by neighborhood residents shall be provided.
>
> Where financial problems are a barrier to effective participation, financial assistance (e.g., babysitting fees, reimbursement for transportation, compensating for serving on Boards or Committees) should be extended to neighborhood residents to assure their opportunity to participate.
>
> Neighborhood residents will be employed in the planning activities and in the execution of the program, with a view toward development of new career lines, including appropriate training and modification of local civil service regulations for entry and promotion."[12]

The city is required to establish a resident component with the CDA to provide "the means for the Model Neighborhood's citizens to participate and be fully involved in policy-making, planning and the execution of all program elements."

A critical examination of these performance standards reveals that they are rather open-ended. They are permissive rather than restrictive, suggestive rather than prescriptive. It might well be that this was exactly what the policy makers intended. Cities developing participation structures under the guidelines of these performance standards would not be bound to any real definition of what level of participation should be attained or allowed. But, the kind of level of participation allowed and/or attained would be shaped according to a number of variables -- including the political forces and administrative structure of the city, the political sophistication and cohesiveness of the model neighborhood residents (which might take into account their previous experience with the OEO war on poverty programs). The significance of these performance standards lies in the long-run implications for the distribution of decision-making power and resource allocation at the neighborhood level. The short-run impact and implication is greatly lessened by the absence of definite compliance regulations.

Federal language on resident participation in Model Cities, then lends itself to varying operational definitions. However, generally speaking, "resident participation" might be understood as the actions of Model Neighborhood residents which affect the control and structure of the program as well as the process through which decisions are made.

Melvin Mogulof gives us some insights into the schizophrenic nature of resident participation. He notes that the history of federal participation policy have developed without a very clear picture of the problem, and, just as important, without a consensus of what role citizen participation should play in the various federal programs.[13] To some social scientists and federal administrators, citizen participation was seen as a way of not alienating the poor and disadvantaged in the planning and delivery of social services. To some extent this was entertained as a possible solution to meeting the increasing demands of minorities for a redistribution of decision-making authority. For others, resident participation was seen as a possible strategy for building an effective political constituency for new social programs designed to deal with poverty and its victims.

But citizen participation in both the CAP program and in Model Cities have been unique in the history of Federal programs. Participation in these programs has focused on the building of structures to insure continuous sensitivity to the issues of governance as opposed to the transient, single purpose involvement of the "Blue Ribbon" and volunteer committees of the past. As we have noted, both of these programs have been influenced to a large degree by the "reform movement" described in previous chapters. One of the carry-overs of this influence has been the programs' concern with the problems of poverty, and specifically with that category of persons referred to as the "powerless" living within a specified area. The structure for citizen participation in these two programs is, in theory, meant to provide an on-going mechanism for influencing a redistribution, or a restructuring of "power" or influence in decision-making to benefit the "powerless" who reside with the target areas. Given this characteristic, community action agencies and the Model City agencies represent a potentially viable governmental structure able to continuously offer the "powerless" opportunities to influence the decisions made within the aegis of these programs.

Citizen Participation Structures

For the sake of simplicity we are viewing resident participation as those activities carried out by residents to affect the control and process through which decisions are made. Naturally, the style and extent of resident participation can vary as a function of the intensity of resident activity in the major operational phases of the program: planning, operation and development.

The "intensity of resident activity" is a factor that is dependent on many variables with the Model Cities action arena. One of these variables is the organizational structure of the participatory mechanism itself. James Sundquist noted that cities tended to choose one of two main forms of resident participation structures, depending on the level of prior organization within the resident neighborhood. These two forms are classified as "bicameral" and "unicameral".[14] Cities where a high degree of organization existed appeared to have preferred a "bicameral structure". This structure called for an independent neighborhood organization (independent of the city demonstration agency) which would participate in developing and reviewing program proposals in more-or-less equal partnership with the city's public and private agencies. In cities where the poor had been unorganized or less assertive, the Model Cities plan embodied a unicameral structure within which the neighborhood residents and the agency representative joined in a single planning process.

Sundquist's organizational models suggest that residents' influence on the programs' operations would be stronger under a bicameral rather than a unicameral scheme. But this did not necessarily mean that the several power issues remained a closed matter after settling on a particular participatory structure. The "power issues" remain;[15] under the bicameral organizational scheme, how many seats would be allocated to representatives of the neighborhood on the policy-making board (assuming the CDA were to be governed by this board) -- a majority, a substantial minority, a small minority or none at all? How would

the neighborhood representative be chosen -- by the mayor or the CDA, by existing neighborhood organizations, or through an election process? In a unicameral
system, what would be the relationship of the residents to the professional
staff of the CDA and other agencies in the planning process? In a bicameral
structure, how would the neighborhood organization be formed? Would it have
its own staff of advocate planners? What would be its role in development of
proposals for inclusion in the city's plan? Would it have veto power over the
proposals of the professionals? If not, how would disputes be settled?

Several students of resident participation have developed scales or
categories of participation. These scales indicate the amount of resident influence in social intervention programs which attempt to involve residents in
their operation. At one end of the spectrum there exists a situation where the
prescribed activity of the residents does not affect the operational process of
the program in any significant degree. Usually, this type of participation
limits the activity of residents; in this role they are "educated" and "placated"
without having a substantial and defined responsibility. At the other end of
the spectrum, the activity of the residents is the controlling influence on the
program's operation. Here the residents are given a substantial role in the
policy and managerial aspects of the program and are able to negotiate the conditions under which "outsiders" may change them.

Sherry Arnstein called her model "the eight rungs on the ladder of
citizen participation". In this model, she presents a self-styled "provocative
typology" of citizen participation, which ranges from "manipulation" (non-
participation) to citizen control (participation with delegated resident power).[16]
In a review entitled "Neighborhood Power and Control", Speigle and Mittenthal
developed a similar participatory scale,[17] ranging from information, consultation, delegation of planning responsibility and neighborhood control. The
Oakland Task Force of the San Francisco Federal Executive Board developed a
scale ranging in intensity from employment, through dialogue and influence, to
control. Mogulof combines the latter two scales and comes up with four measures
of intensity (ranging from "least" to "most" intense): a) employment - information; b) dialogue - advice giving; c) shared authority; d) control.[18] Other
students have developed similar scales, including Marshall Kaplan, whose consulting firm has been hired by HUD to monitor the planning process in the Model
City Program. The following chart is a comparative depiction of some of these
typologies:

Comparative Typologies of Resident Participation

Sherri Arnstein	Hans Speigel	James Sundquist	Marshall Kaplan
Manipulation	Information	Unicameral/CDA Control	Staff Dominance/ Resident Legitimation
Therapy	Consultation	Bicameral/City Hall-Oriented	Staff Influence/ Resident Sanction
Informing	Negotiation	Bicameral/ Unified	
Consultation	Shared Policy		Staff/Resident Parity
Placation	Joint Planning	Bicameral/ Neighborhood Oriented	
Partnership	Delegation of Planning Responsibility		Resident Influence/ Staff Sanction
Delegated Power			
Citizen Control	Neighborhood Control	Resident Control	Resident Dominance/ Staff Legitimation

In most of the hundred and fifty model cities programs, a considerable amount of time and energy has been expended in negotiating, defining, redefining, and fashioning citizen participation structures. However, the rights and responsibilities of the various boards, committees and task forces are often less defined and sadly ambiguous. This ambiguity, partly attributable to lack of compliance regulations from HUD, resulted in considerable conflict during the program's operation. At some point, residents seemed to realize that their part in "widespread participation" had not extended beyond the point where the power-holders have decided to placate them.

Arnstein cites the result of a study which questions the operational effectiveness of "widespread citizen participation".[19] The findings are as follows:

1. Most CDA's did not negotiate citizen participation requirements with residents.

2. Citizens, drawing on past negative experiences with local power-holders, were extremely suspicious of this new program. They were legitimately distrustful of city hall's motives.

3. Most CDA's were not working with citizens' groups that were representative of model neighborhoods and accountable to neighborhood constituencies. As in so many of the poverty programs, those who were involved were more representative of the upwardly mobile working class. Thus, their acquiescence to plans prepared by city agencies was not likely to reflect the views of the unemployed, the young, the more militant residents, and the hard core poor.

4. Residents who were participating in as many as three to five meetings per week were unaware of their minimum rights, responsibilities and the options available to them under the program. For example, they did not realize that they were not required to accept technical help from city technicians they distrusted.

5. Most of the technical assistance provided by CDA's and the city agencies was of third-rate quality, paternalistic and condescending. Agency technicians did not suggest innovative options. They reacted bureaucratically when residents pressed for innovative approaches. The vested interest of the old-line city agencies were a major, albeit hidden, agenda.

6. Most CDA's were not engaged in planning that was comprehensive enough to expose and deal with the roots of urban decay. They engaged in "meetingitis" and were supporting strategies that resulted in "projectitis", the outcome of which was a "laundry list" of traditional programs to be conducted by traditional agencies in the traditional manner.

7. Residents were not getting enough information from CDA's to enable them to review CDA developed plans or to initiate plans of their own as required by HUD. At best, they were getting copies of official HUD materials.

8. Most residents were unaware of their rights to be reimbursed for expenses incurred because of participation -- babysitting, transportation cost, and so on.

9. The training of residents, which would enable them to understand the labyrinth of the federal-state-city system and networks of the subsystems, was an item that most CDA's did not even consider.

Arnstein further cites the results of this evaluation carried out by OSTI, a private consulting firm based in Cambridge, Massachusetts. OSTI's report not only underscored the earlier study, but went on further to say:

"in practically no Model Cities structure does citizen
participation mean truly shared decision-making, such
that citizens might view themselves as 'the partners in
this program....'"[20]

Interest of Minorities and the Model Cities Program

As stated earlier, Model Cities proposes a comprehensive and coordinated attack on poverty in the "hard core" slums of several American cities.
Slums have increasingly become the dwelling place of ethnic minorities. These
people have been traditionally excluded from substantive participation in the
politics and benefits of the American society, especially in the politics of
decisions that affect their daily lives. It is therefore not surprising that
resident participation has become the dominant issue in the Model Cities experience. Model Cities could not avoid the momentum of the Civil Rights, Black
Power, and other social movements that had the underlying premise of community
control high on their agendas. Resident participation in Model Cities has
increasingly become an issue around which racial confrontation between black
residents and white municipal power structures have taken place. As a framework for analysis it would be appropriate to contrapose the city and the neighborhood as contending parties in the Model Cities political process.[21] Each
has its respective goals, strategies, and ideologies which are in most cases
non-parallel. In addition, both are engaged over an indefinite period in a
competition for control of program resources; and it is this political process
which ultimately structures interaction between the two groups.

In context of such an analysis, Model Cities and their CDA's across
the country are faced with an inevitable dilemma of conflicting allegiance to
City Halls and to neighborhood groups. It has been almost impossible for a
CDA to serve both since the neighborhood is not likely to trust an agency that
services City Hall. For CDA's the basic political question becomes how to
reconcile the needs of city hall for a coordinating mechanism and the interest
and demands of neighborhood groups.

Thus, resident participation has emerged as a powerful reality that
has changed the entire conception of what the planning process would be like
and what goals might be accomplished.[22] The issues of control and accountability to the interest of area residents have dominated most of the events in
the Model Cities experience. An evaluative report by Marshall Kaplan, Gans and
Kahn, a private consulting firm, indicates that during the application period,

the issues generated by the Program were largely concerned with Model Neighborhood boundaries and the role of residents in the anticipated CDA structure. During the initial months of the planning period, the prominent issues were related primarily to area residents' relationships to structure and definition of planning roles.[23]

The demand for greater participation or community control derives its credibility from the experience of poor and racial minorities in urban America. Let us take the issue of education as an example. The parents and residents of "hard core" slums have pressed for real education for years, going through the entire range of challenges and responses, from desegregation to compensatory programs. Still, neither the achievement level of their children nor opportunities for better education have improved. The statistics of the 1970 census corroborate this assertion: about half of all black teenagers are in school, and most of these are obviously not in the labor force. Of those not in school, nearly two in every ten are unemployed and four in ten are neither at work nor can find work. Additionally there is a significant number of those out of school who are keeping house, dying on the front lines of the Vietnam War, or working without pay in the family business or farm. As a whole, the black unemployment rate in 1970 was about eight percent -- much higher than the white rate.[24]

Their conclusion: bureaucracy, the white power structure, is not sincerely interested in improving the lot of minority poor. Their goal now becomes to make the local institutions accountable to them, the people whom these institutions are supposed to serve. The issue is the quality and relevance of local institutions to local needs, and they see the present fight for real participation as only a current phase of a long struggle against a system they deem at the least unresponsive and at most simply racist.

On the other hand, those that constitute the bureaucratic power structure, personnel and leaders, have their own unique life experiences. These are experiences which have led them to have an automatic respect for existing social institutions which people in "hard core" slums feel have failed them miserably: whether governmental, educational, professional, or other, these institutions respond to centralized power centers extremely remote from the world of the inner city. What happens to these residents is determined by others -- by the white power structure, and consequently they feel powerless in controlling their own destiny.

As for the residents of the "hard core" slums, they want what all Americans want: quality education, effective social services, responsible police, liveable housing, dignified work, adequate income, and a pleasant living environment. They are demanding no more than their white counterparts in the suburbs or more exclusive city neighborhoods, who for years have controlled the institutions which affect their lives.

Given the dynamics described above, it is understandable why black people and other minority groups should view intervention efforts such as Model Cities with great suspicion. Some community leaders regard these efforts as attempts to subterfuge "community control: under the guise of promises to redevelop "hard core slums." To a great degree, these fears and frustrations are valid. Urban renewal slum clearance projects, highway construction projects, and large social intervention projects have all contributed to these frustrations. They have inconvenienced the poor to benefit the affluent, and caused considerable dissension within the communities themselves.

The sad truth is that black and other minorities have no basis for trust and confidence in white dominated institutions. In a sense the call for greater participation is a call for accountability, demanding the right to make the same mistakes on their own behalf that federal, state, and local governments have been making for them.[25] At minimum, the participation movement is a call to redirect public policy so that it would be more amenable and sensitive to the needs of the groups they affect most.

The anxieties and potential threat which "participation" conjures up in the eyes of urban chief executives constitutes one of the major barriers of effective resident participation. It is assumed on some levels that if ethnic minorities are charged with the responsibilities of management control and given decision-making powers, the inevitable result would be fiscal shortages, "Hate Whitey" campaigns underwritten with federal dollars, and alleged revolutionary and paramilitary activity. In addition, there exists considerable paranoia on the part of policy makers when called on to lend support to minorities, since the powerless tend to strike against those who parade themselves as their champions.[26]

On the other side of the fence, there are students of the participation issue who have viewed the resident participation allowed in Model Cities with a sense of cynicism and negativism equal to that of ethnic minority groups. They allege that "widespread citizen participation" seems to have objectives that:

1. Help to reduce tension in the ghettos by giving residents a feeling that they are gaining power in community-level decision making.

2. Assures the existing agencies that resident participation would not require them to change in any basic way, not threaten any of the major programs.

3. Gives citizens the illusion that they are participating in major decisions, but harbors assurances that their participation would be relatively meaningless, and would not affect program development in any drastic way.

4. Convince many third parties—the federal agencies, the "man-in-the-street," the press, the legislature—that you have really given "wide-spread citizen participation" a fair trial.

5. Accounts for any failure of a program as owing to the inaptitude of low-income citizen participation.[27]

There are other students who question the effectiveness of resident participation as the mechanism for dealing with the powerlessness of the ghetto residents. The concern here is that resident participation is ineffective if preliminary work is not done in the larger community to prepare for its success. Irwin Lazar points out that while middle-class people can form around a social issue and be confident that their unity will give them strength, that their membership can mobilize public opinion and that together they can influence social decisions, the poor do not share this confidence. He concludes with a note of pessimism: "the only action by the poor 'we' have enforced has been riots."[28] Providing a grounding on the sociology of groups in the American experience, Lazar observes that the poor are not, by and large, the most active community group members. Community activity is more likely to be taken up by the upwardly mobile who can afford the time and energy. The poorest members of the community are usually too busy struggling to survive. It is unreasonable, given this reality, to expect "wide-spread citizen participation" among the poor until their basic needs are met.[29]

It should be noted that the poorer members of the "hard-core slums" at times view the upwardly mobile as having negative middle-class values. Since the middle-class minority group members characteristically assume positions of political leadership as a result of social mobility, they are at times all too eager to forget their lower class heritage. The negative result is that the "oppressed" tends to identify with the "oppressor", consequently turning harsh, punitive and authoritarian in their treatment of the poor people they have been charged with representing.

Despite all of these "short comings" resident participation remains a dynamic force whose course will not be rerouted. Moreover, any intervention effort to deal with the problems of poverty without a viable resident participation mechanism could be seriously undermined.

Edgar Cahn, a well known advocate for citizen participation in social intervention programs, identified the following values of resident participation as justifiable and rational reasons for its continual operationalization:

1. A means of mobilizing unutilized resources--A source of productivity and labor not otherwise tapped.

2. A source of knowledge--Both corrective and creative. A means of securing feedback regarding policy and program and also a source of new, innovative approaches.

3. An end in itself--An affirmation of democracy aiming at the elimination of alienation, and the combatting of destructiveness, hostility and cynicism.

4. Guarantee of a social contract--In as much as minority residents claim they do not have any basis for trusting white dominated institutions, real participation offers a mechanism through which trust can be developed. It is a guarantee, frail as it may be, that people will be willing to endorse the terms of the social contract--and to have sufficient faith in the system to work within its limits.

5. Guarantee (of sorts) for the Pursuit of Equality--In as much as the "system" gives the poor what "it" judges they should want, "it" is not structured to challenge the basic pattern of segregation and inequality. The "system" and "its" officials are charged with the delicate responsibility of appropriately allocating limited resources; they must set the priorities based on research, documentation and policy formulation. The important point residents emphasize is that the officials do not have to bear the burden of living with the choices they make, based on research, documentation and policy formulation.

6. Creating a Neighborhood power force--Given the character of powerlessness of minorities in the urban centers, real participation offers a mechanism through which they can create a base of power to influence the distribution of resources.

7. Vehicle for political socialization--Real participation provides access to interaction with governmental and community influentials, and thus contributing to the political education of minority groups.

8. Vehicle for positive role perception--The impact on the increased sense of self-identity and pride on minority is in and of itself a positive value of real participation.

Contextual Summation of the Issues in Resident Participation

In previous chapters an attempt has been made to outline the historical and sociological development of "resident participation". As a conceptual framework, the sociology of knowledge allowed us to view the conflicting dynamics of the issues raised by the "reform movement" in theoretical terms. In tracing the development of "citizen participation", several important principles have been recognized:

a. American Society and its institutions were seen as in part responsible for the fact that 30 million Americans live in abject poverty.

b. As a strategy to combat poverty, determined efforts were made to create a sense of community among the "powerless" groups.

c. In conjunction with the latter, it was concluded that the "powerless" had to be given some compensatory leverage to petition their grievances against the institutions of society. It is on this basis that the phrases "maximum feasible participation of the poor" and "widespread citizen participation" emerged.

The eventual demise of the "reform movement" which sanctioned the above principles is partially associated with the raise of black nationalism and the call for self-determination (community control) by the "powerless" in a number of urban ghettos. This occurred when those who were seen as "powerless" engaged the resources of a federal intervention program to assert their "power" and at times seemed to threaten existing institutions and the local governments themselves. These events alerted and influenced the authors of the Model Cities program. Taking into account the political controversy engendered by previous programs, Model Cities policy makers were reluctant to bestow their programs with similar formats. One of the more important changes reflected in the Model Cities program was a rejection of the strategy of establishing a new institution outside the system, such as the Community Action Agencies. It was decided that for this new effort local governments would be charged with the primary responsibility of the program's operation. Robert Wood, head of the Model Cities Task Force, articulated the premise on which this change was made, when he stated:

> "...I am not willing to embrace the simple injection of money as an exclusive response to urban ills, or to abandon the task of changing and strengthening public institutions, especially those at the local level. Six years of participation in the national government makes me less sanguine that Washington can carry the total burden of urban reform or respond to the genuine cry for citizen participation in local affairs. Accordingly, I focus more strongly on devising common activities and emphasizing common purposes at the metropolitan level to enable a continental democracy to respond more flexibly and rapidly to the needs of its 200 million citizens."[30]

Thus a new institution - the City Demonstration Agency - was created to expand the leadership role of the mayor over the program. This event created some problems for effective citizen participation as seen from the perspective of the "powerless". Additionally it placed some constraints on the agency itself in identifying and promoting their concerns. The director of the CDA is placed in the conflicting position of being both the Mayor's man and at the same time the citizen's advocate. As a result, in most instances, the prescribed mechanisms for instituting resident participation in the Model Cities Program have also conflicted with the increasing demands of ethnic minorities for a more substantive role in the operation and development of the program.

Inherent conflict has also evolved between national planning and coordination of urban resources as a goal and "effective" citizen participation as a goal. The CDA director, who is directly responsible to the mayor or city manager must be oriented toward program results and efficiency. His overall responsibility is to deliver a program goods and services as quickly and efficiently as possible. (His definition of both "efficiency" and "goods and services" may, of course, be at variance with that of the intended recipient). It is in this respect that some students[31] of "resident participation" have seen the conflict in terms of "production vs. participation".[32] Accordingly, it could be argued that there is an inverse relationship between the degree and strength of citizen participation and the production of program results.

Extending the implication of these conflicts further, we can see that those residents of the urban ghettos who have taken up the banner of community control might well be at odds with the Model Cities programs' notion of "efficiency" in citizen participation. On the one hand the CDA director is concerned with program efficiency. He therefore sees the function of resident participation as a supportive role which would enhance the flow of services. On the other hand the resident advocate of community control is not as concerned with program efficiency as defined by the city. He is concerned with increased influence in the program's operation. Hence he sees the function of resident participation as a mechanism to redistribute power.

The dynamics of these conflicts is captured in an event cited by Hans B. C. Speigel. A black spokesman for the local model neighborhood residents is being urged to consult with city hall on some contentious issues. The spokesman response is:

> "The time has passed for me that I will be defined by you or
> others like you and be told what is reasonable by folks like
> you... Whether you agree or not, Congress and City Halls
> around the country are the enemy of the poor because they
> control the public institutions which oppress many of the
> poor. And if the poor happen to be black, the oppression
> seems more acceptable and rational. That kind of polarity
> existed before my time and will in all probability continue
> after my time.... The problem is to recognize a polarity
> and move toward a bargaining situation in which the interest
> of parties in conflict can be negotiated. I intend that the
> representatives of the black community of the poor in West
> Oakland approach that situation with a strong bargaining posi-
> tion with hat on head and not in hand..."[33]

Participation which would only allow the neighborhood residents to "advise" the Model Cities agency rather than to control a part of the planning, operation, and development of the program appears unacceptable to ethnic minority group leadership. But obviously no Model Cities program can meet the criteria for complete resident control since final approval power and accountability rest with each city government. The recent historical trend of federal citizen participation policies, in addition and concomitant to the civil rights and community control movements, all point to "control" as the logical and needed extension of the participation concept. Given this reality, the critical questions of the participation issues are: <u>how is resident participation unfolding in the ghettos of urban areas? How does the decision making processes which have evolved in the Model Cities Program relate to ethnic minority demands for increased influence in decision making?</u>

Specifically, have ethnic minority groups been able to use the participation mechanisms in the Model City program to resolve their sense of powerlessness? And if so, under what conditions?

Although there has been an abundance of literature and studies on citizen participation, there have been few hard empirical findings concerning these questions. The aim of this study is to provide such an empirical study. I am concerned that, for an issue so currently important to the "have-nots", there has been little attempt to coordinate data useful to their planning for a greater role in their communities.

The central thrust of this study is therefore to examine whether measures of resident participation in the Model Cities program make it possible to predict the extent of influence residents are likely to gain the programs operation. It is anticipated that the higher the intensity of resident participatory activity, the more significant will be the degree of resident influence in the program's operation. In keeping with the more usual model in social science, the overall null hypothesis--namely, that there is no relationship between participation and control--will be tested.

Footnotes - Chapter III:

1. Sundquist, James. Making Federalism Work, "A Study of Program Coordination at the Community Level," The Brookings Institution, 1970, p. 80.

2. Model Cities Service Center Bulletin, A Report on Progress (special issue), Vol. 2, No. 9 - 1971, p. 4.

3. Bulletin, op. cit., p. 6.

4. Ibid., p. 5.

5. Bulletin, p. 5-6.

6. Mogulof, Melvin. "Citizen Participation: A Review and Commentary on Federal Policies and Practices," Working Paper: 102-111, The Urban Institute, Washington, 1970. Daniel P. Moynihan, op. cit., also observed and documented evidence to this effect. He noted (p. 185) that when the Johnson Administration put together the Model Cities program, it was provided that local communities would be allowed to participate in the planning process, but strictly in association with the local government. Thus, the policy makers of the Model Cities program had no intention of letting what happened with the Gray areas and Community Action's Programs happen with Model Cities.

7. Model Cities Program Guide, Chapter I.

8. Sundquist, op. cit., p. 101.

9. Letter, Andrew J. Bell, III, Assistant Regional Administer, HUD Region VI, to the Honorable Joseph L. Alioto, February 4, 1970.

10. Letter, Floyde Hyde, Assistant Secretary for Model Cities, to Alfonso J. Dervantes, January 9, 1970.

11. Sherry Arnstein and Daniel Fox, paper - "Technical Assistance Paper on Citizen Participation," Department of Housing and Urban Development - July 8, 1968.

12. CDA Letter No. 3, "Citizen Participation," MCGR 3100.3, November, 1967, paragraph 3. The information found below comes from Melvin Mogulof's Citizen Review, Chapter I.

13. Melvin Mogulof, op. cit., p. 2.

14. Sundquist, op. cit., pp. 86-88.

15. Ibid., p. 86-88.

16. Sherry Arnstein,"Eight Rungs on the Ladder of Citizen Participation," AIP Journal, p. 216, July, 1969.

17. Mogulof, op. cit., p. 4-5.

18. Ibid., p. 6.

19. Arnstein, op. cit., p. 220.

20. Arnstein, Sherry, op. cit., p. 222.

21. Mittenthal, Steve, dissertation; "Resident Power, Implications of Planning and Community Control." He uses this dichotomy as a basis for analysis.

22. Brooks, Michael, "Social Planning and City Planning." ASPO publication which presents a comprehensive review of the complex subject of social planning and a critical examination of the profession's most significant response to social problems to date -- advocacy planning.

23. The Model Cities Program, Department of Housing and Urban Development, Washington, D.C., p. 65.

24. "Black Americans", a chartbook, U. S. Department of Labor, Bureau of Statistics, Bulletin 1699, 1971.

25. Alan Alshuler, Community Control: The Black Demand for Participation in Large American Cities, New York, pegasus, p. 14.

26. Cahn, Edgar, Passet, Barry, editors. Citizen Participation: Effective Community Change. Praeger Special Studies in U.S. Economic and Social Development, New York, pp. 15-16.

27. Warren, Roland, The Model Cities Program: "Assumptions--Experience-- Implications," paper presented at the Annual Forum Program, National Conference on Social Welfare, Dallas, Texas, May 17, 1971.

28. Cahn, Edgar, Passett, Barry, op. cit., pp. 92-109.

29. Cahn, op. cit., p. 111.

30. Warren, Roland, editor, Politics and The Ghettos, p. 81.

31. Hans Speigel, "Citizen Participation in Federal Programs - A Review", Journal of Voluntary Action Research, monograph #1, 1971, p. 7.

32. Ibid, p. 8.

33. Hans Speigel, op. cit., p. 9.

CHAPTER IV

METHODOLOGY

Introduction

The major data resource for this research effort is a series of
chronological case histories compiled and written by Marshall, Kaplan, Gans,
and Khan (MKGK), a private consulting firm based in San Francisco, California.
At the onset of the Model Cities Program, MKGK was contracted by the Model
Cities Administration of the Department of Housing and Urban Development (HUD)
to conduct an evaluation of the Model Cities Program during its first two
years of operation.[1] The purpose of the study was to provide policy-makers
with analyses which could be used to alter, amend, redirect, or emphasize
policy for the Model Cities Program. In addition, MKGK hoped to distill from
its examination of Model Cities lessons applicable to the solution of urban
problems in general. Because the reliability and validity of this study are in-
extricably tied to that of the MKGK evaluation, a description of the firm's
methodology is presented here.

The MKGK research design was based on the development of a series of
chronological case histories of the first two years of Model Cities activity in
eleven of the cities where first-round Model Cities Programs were funded. The
selection of cities for inclusion in the study was conducted jointly with the
staff of HUD's Model Cities Administration and was based on a conscientious
effort to choose cities with characteristics considered both representative of
most American cities and essential to an understanding of the impact of the
Model Cities Program on local communities. MKGK designed and implemented a
systematic monitoring process for the collection of data. Each of the eleven
cities was assigned a trained evaluator from the MKGK staff who visited the
city for at least one week each month during the two-year period under study.
In addition, MKGK employed local personnel in each of the cities who were
closely affiliated with Model Cities activities and who provided the MKGK
evaluator's absence.

At the end of the second year of Model Cities funding, the information
collected through this monitoring process was compiled to form a chronological
case history for each of the eleven cities. The purpose of these chronologies
was to provide a reliable, continuous history both of the Model Cities program

in each city and of the range of interaction among municipal staff, HUD regional personnel, local service institutions, and the local residents. Although focused primarily on recounting the activities of the City Demonstration Agencies, the chronologies also record the activities of other social intervention programs operating in the city and events (such as city elections, or riots) which either should have or did impact in any way on the Model Cities Program. In addition, specific attention was paid to developing an accurate picture of the political cohesiveness of the Model Neighborhood residents. The topics with which the MKGK evaluation was concerned and which are covered in the chronologies include:

1. Planning activities;
2. Evaluation activities;
3. Timetables of submission of planning products to HUD;
4. The review process by HUD;
5. Influence of HUD requirements on the local programs operations;
6. Leadership and intervention by the local municipal chief;
7. Residents role in the planning process and program implementation;
8. Background of CDA director and key staff members (race, education, prior experience, personality factors. Relations with other actors);
9. Relations between chief executive and CDA director/staff and citizens;
10. Relations between CDA director/staff and citizens;
11. Relations with federal, state and local agencies and their programs;
12. Roles of non-Model Cities actors;
13. Training and technical assistance;
14. The particular subject areas which were monitored closely, viz; housing, education, health and relocation; and,
15. Evaluation of CDA Board and resident organization leadership.

In addition, in order to establish the context in which the events included in the chronology occurred, each one contains an introductory background chapter describing the city, its people, economy, government and its previous experience with Federal programs.

Data Collection

As has already been pointed out, the chronologies constitute a source of secondary data for this study. During the academic year 1970-1971, as a part of his internship, the author was assigned to the MKGK staff to work on its Model Cities evaluation team. It was during this internship that he systematically gathered data on the eleven first-round cities, and was responsible for monitoring, editing and developing a classification scheme for the resident-participation related events reported in the chronologies.

While case studies have been widely used as a method of analysis, they have not always been considered "proper" methodology as an exclusive instrument since they do not permit generalization beyond the situation and actors described. The set of MKGK chronologies, however, are not so constrained, since the focus on the CDA, its activities, and other related events affecting the program was consistent throughout the evaluation study. Certainly one of the constant aspects of the program was activity stimulated by the "widespread citizen participation" requirement. Given that this is the area of interest of this study, a methodology which could provide the information required to assess the degree of influence the MNA residents were able to exercise in each of the eleven programs was highly desirable. To this end, the first step in this research effort was to read each chronology in its entirety to screen out the observable variations in the degree of influence MNA residents were able to exercise in the program's operation. The first reading of the chronologies also revealed some of the variant factors which seemed to be associated with different degrees of influence exercised by the residents. The literature on citizen participation and interviews conducted with key Model Cities administrators supported observations gleaned from the chronologies. These preliminary procedures indicated that there were some variables which might be related to the intensity of resident activity, and therefore to a greater resident influence in the program. The variables selected for analysis were those that were observable within the scope of the chronologies and that lent themselves to reliable operationalization.

A data collection schedule was constructed to systematically collect data from each chronology. This schedule functioned as an interviewer, treating each chronology as the interviewer respondent. In this manner, data assumed to have bearing on resident participation and control were collected. A copy of this data collection instrument can be found in Appendix A.

In order to facilitate the analysis of the data, three sets of variables were identified:

... Intervening variables

... Independent variables

... Dependent variables

It is anticipated that an analysis of the association between the variables identified in the chronologies will give answers to the principal questions raised by this research effort.

Intervening Variables

The relationship between the activities undertaken by the residents as a result of the Model Cities Program and the degree of influence they were able to exercise is varied and complex. Similar resident activity can yield dissimilar results among different types of individuals and within different environments. This research effort seeks to extend the chain of causation by treating as intervening variables the governmental type of the city, population size of the city, organizational cohesiveness of the local residents, ethnic composition of the city, and the extent of racial disturbances (if any) which occurred in the city prior to or during the Model Cities Program.

Two sets of intervening variables have been identified. The first, labeled Environment I, includes the population size of the city, type of municipal government, racial composition of the city and that of the MNA. The second, labeled Environment II, includes indices of racial conflict in the city occurring either during the two years prior to the Model Cities Program or during the two year period studied by MKGK. This subset also includes a measure of the political cohesiveness of the MNA residents vis-a-vis the Model Cities Program.

While it may be argued that these variables do not exhaust the environmental factors associated with the degree and extent of control which might be attained by residents in a given locality, they do consistently and substantively characterize the locale of each of the programs studied. Whereas Environment I identifies the city from a broad population and political organizational perspective, Environment II seeks to more explicitly identify the degree of overt racial hostility which might have occurred in that city and the cohesiveness of the minority population.

OPERATIONALIZATION OF INTERVENING VARIABLES

Var #1	Size of City	1=Large (above 325,000); 2=Medium (between 150,000-325,000); 3=Small (under 150,000).
Var #2	Type of Municipal Government	1=Strong Mayor; 2=Commission or City Manager with Mayor elected at large; 3= City Manager with Weak Mayor.
Var #3	Race and Ethnic Composition of City	1-Large (above 30%); 2=Medium (between 15-30%); 3=Small (below 15%).
Var #4	Race and Ethnic Composition of MNA	1-Large (above 60%); 2=Medium (between 20-60%); 3=Small (below 20%).

With respect to Variable No. 1, larger cities (where ethnic minorities were greater in numbers) received a higher rating than smaller cities.

Under the rationale for Variable No. 2, cities with strong mayors received a lower rating than city-manager-run cities. The assumption here was that MNA residents would be more likely to be influential and active in cities which have a decentralized governmental structure, for such structures tend to be less sensitive to partisan political influence in their administrative organization.[2]

Similar ordinal rationales were used for Variables Nos. 3 and 4: Cities with large ethnic minority population were rated higher than those with small ethnic populations. (The definition of ethnic minorities included both Black and Spanish-surname peoples). The reasoning here was that the ethnic minority residents would be more active and influential in cities where their number are greater.

Var #5	Racial Conflict in the city/MNA prior to Model Cities	1=Major conflict; 2=Medium conflict; 3= Small conflict.
Var #6	Racial Conflict in the City/MNA during Model Cities	1=Major conflict; 2=Medium conflict; 3= Small conflict.
Var #7	Organizational Cohesiveness	1-Very cohesive; 2=General cohesive; 3= Minimally cohesive.

The rationale used for scaling Variables Nos. 5 and 6 is similar to that used by the Kerner Commission to classify the magnitude of riots which occurred in the United States. Taken into consideration are the number of victims killed as a result of the riot, the number of people injured and the extent of physical damage in the city/MNA.

The measurement of Variable No. 7 was based on the reported presence of active community organizations in the Model Cities locality; the degree of community and extra-organizational interaction and cooperation displayed by the community organizations; and the extent to which the organizations interacted among themselves in regards to the Model Cities Program.

OPERATIONALIZATION OF THE INDEPENDENT VARIABLES

Var #8	Resident Involvement in the Application Period	1=Very Active; 2=Mild; 3=No involvement.
Var #9	Resident Activity for Increase Role in the M.C. process	1=Strong; 2=Active; 3=Mild
Var #10	Resident Participation in selection of CDA Directors	1=Active; 2=Mild; 3=No.

| Var #11 | Representativeness of resident structures of neighborhood constituency | 1=Very; 2=Generally; 3=Not. |

| Var #12 | Directors sympathy with community control | 1=Strong; 2=Mild; 3=No. |

| Var #13 | Role of Residence in designing CDA structure | 1=Active; 2=Mild; 3=No. |

| Var #14 | Structure of Resident Body | 1=Separate; 2=Within "CDA". |

| Var #15 | Role of Residents in Establishing Prerrogatives of C.P. Structure | 1=Active; 2=Mild; 3=No. |

| Var #16 | Percentage of Ethnic Minorities on C.P. Structure | 1=Dominant (60% or greater; 2=Equity (40-59%); 3=Inequity (40%). |

| Var #17 | Information flow from CDA to Resident Structure | 1=Good; 2=Average; 3=Poor. |

| Var #18 | Extent of Professional Cooperation with Residents | 1=Strong; 2=General; 3=Low. |

Independent Variables

The independent variables measure those program activities undertaken either by residents or CDA staff resultant from the award and operationalization of a Model Cities grant in a locality. These variables (identified in the literature and chronologies) constitute actual measures of resident participation, the activities undertaken by the CDA staff to insure effective resident participation, and the pre-conditions necessary for effective participation.

Var #8 ... <u>Resident Involvement in the Application Phase for a Model Cities Grant</u>

To what extent and how were residents included in the locality's application for a Model Cities grant? During the application phase, a considerable amount of organizational, structural and operational program planning occurs. Thus meaningful resident input is critical if the program is to emphasize resident participation during its later developmental and operational stages. This variable, then, provides a general measure of a city's attempts to integrate the inputs of residents in the development of the program's application. Cities where residents participated in these activities and where their participation significantly influenced the issues considered and decisions made were rated "active". Ratings of "mild" were given to those cities whose resident participation during the application phase was pro forma, i.e., resident's influence was limited to making amendments, giving advice, or sanctioning decisions which were already made by the CDA. Cities received a rating of "no" if resident participation at this stage did not result in meaningful contributions to the grant application.

Var #9 ... Indices of Resident Activity for an Increased Role in the Model Cities Process

Were residents satisfied with the established structures of the Model Cities Program (the CDA structure, the resident participation structure); and/or with their relative roles in the programmatic development during the two-year period under study? If not, what action(s) did they take to ensure adequate representation of their interest. This variable attempts to measure the relative satisfaction of Model Neighborhood residents with the established organizational structures and processes governing the operation of the program. It provides an index of stability, reflecting satisfaction or the dissatisfaction of the local residents with particular aspects or decisions in the program and the intensity with which they sought to redress their dissatisfaction. Cities were rated strong on Variable No. 9 if the resident's activity increased their overall influence in the program beyond that previously established by the local Model Cities Administrators. A rating of active was given if the resident's activity was not consistent throughout the two year period, but concentrated around certain issues (on which they were able to exercise significant influence) and/or time periods (review period at the end of the planning year, the waiting period between applications and grant award transition between first planning and first action year periods and HUD regional review periods). Rated <u>mild</u> were those cities in which resident activity to increase their overall influence was sporadic, if at all attempted.

Var #10 ... <u>Resident Participation in the Selection of the CDA Director</u>

How was the CDA Director selected? Was he directly appointed by the local municipal chief, without prior consultation or sanction of some representative body of the Model Neighborhood area; or was he selected by way of a precedural format which integrated the input of a representative body of the Model Neighborhood Area? Although HUD requires that the CDA have a full time director, who with his staff, "will have the overall responsibility for the development and carrying out of the local Model Cities Program,"[3] there is no stipulation for resident input in the selection process for the CDA director. This administrative procedure, like others in the Model Cities Program, is left in large measure to the locality. Ratings of "active," "mild," or "no" were assigned to cities based on the extent of resident participation in the selection of the CDA director and on the degree to which their input was influential in much the same fashion as ratings were assigned on Variable No. 8.

Var #11 ... <u>Representativeness of the Resident Structure of the Neighborhood Constituency</u>

How were the neighborhood representatives chosen? Were they directly appointed by the municipal chief or were they elected through an agreed-upon electoral process? What percentage of the MNA residents voted in the elections? To some extent the degree of representativeness of the resident structure could be seen as a function of the ability of the local residents and their organizations to give priority to their operational unity. Rated "very representative" on Variable No. 11 were those cities which had a relatively high turn out for the resident representatives' elections, and whose resident structures were generally thought to be representative by the residents, community organizations, the media

67

and other groups and individuals as reported by the chronologies.
A rating of "generally representative" was given to those cities
in which the voter turn-out for resident elections was considered
average, and whose resident structure was not viewed as overwhelmingly nonrepresentative by MNA residents and relevant actors
as reported in the chronologies. A rating of "not representative"
was given to those cities whose resident structure was perceived
by the Model Cities staff and a significant number of residents
and relevant actors as not representative as reported in the
chronologies.

Var #12 ... <u>CDA Directors Sympathy to Community Control</u>

The CDA Director in the Model Cities Program plays a pivotal role
between his obligations to the city and the pressures to respond
to the immediate needs of the Model Neighborhood residents. He
could carry out his responsibilities in such a manner that he is
seen singularly as the "mayors boy", and thus alienate to a considerable extent neighborhood demands and concerns and even the Model
Neighborhood residents themselves. The CDA Director could pursue
an administrative posture which (recognizes) and continually
emphasizes the participation of Model Neighborhood residents, thus
using his influence to ensure the continued inputs of residents in
the Model Cities process. This variable, then, measures the CDA
Director's relative advocacy for resident participation. In
addition to specific interviews, with the director and residents,
records of the residents' interaction with the CDA Director around
a variety of the sensitive political decision issues which arose
during the period under study provided the grounding for an index
of the director's sympathy to residents' concerns. A city was
<u>rated strong support</u> on <u>Variable No. 12</u> if the selected CDA
director established himself as an advocate of continued resident
participation in the Model Cities Program both to the city and the
residents. In addition, the director, throughout the two year
period, demonstrated a sensitivity for the residents concerns by
being available to them when critical issues arrived. He became a
fair advocate for their concerns to the city, private agencies and
institutions involved in the Model Cities arena. Cities were rated

<u>mild support</u> if the CDA Director did not explicitly establish himself as a strong advocate for resident participation, but supported resident issues in some instances. On the whole, however, he perceives resident participation within its traditional roles (advisory and revisionary). <u>Rated low support</u> were those cities where the CDA Director did not as a whole support resident issues to the city nor to the agencies involved in the Model Cities arena.

Var #13 ... <u>Role of the Resident in Designing the Prerogatives of the Resident Participation Structure</u>

This variable attempts to determine the extent of residents' influence in structuring the formal prerogatives of the resident participation structure? Were residents given veto power on the final planning products (programs and proposals)? Did they have a definitive role in the planning process? Could the local city council approve programs for funding without prior consultation with the resident group? Ratings of "active," "mild," or "no" were assigned in much the same way as for Variables Nos. 8 and 10.

Var #14 ... <u>Structure of the Resident Participation Body</u>

It has been suggested that the structure of the resident body is an important factor in determining the intensity of resident activity. Was the resident structure independent of the CDA? Did residents participate in developing program proposals in more or less equal partnership with the city's public and private agencies? Or was the resident participation structure organized in such a manner that the neighborhood residents and the agency representatives joined in a single planning process? Variable No. 14 was set up as a dichotomous variable. This proved to be a more manageable way to differentiate the resident structures. If the resident structure was separate from the CDA, the city received a higher rating on this variable than if they were joined together in a single agency.

Var #15 ... <u>Role of the Residents in Designing the Structure and Prerogatives of the CDA Structure</u>

During the application and early planning phases of the Model Cities program, which actors were brought together to design the structure and establish the Prerogatives of the CDA structure and its board, were residents represented? What degree of influence did they have?

Variable No. 15 was measured by the three-point scale of "active", "mild", and "no" used for Variables Nos. 8, 10, and 13.

Var #16 ... <u>Percent of Ethnic Minorities in the Citizen Participation Structure</u>

If the membership of the resident structure was at least 60 percent ethnic minorities, a high rating was given. Middle ratings were assigned to cities where 40 - 59 percent of the persons in this group were members of an ethnic minority; and low ratings were assigned if 39 percent or fewer were members of an ethnic minority.

Var #17 ... <u>Information Flow from the CDA to the Resident Structure</u>

CDA letter #3 states that the resident structure must have clear and direct access to the decision-making process of the CDA in order that the resident structure can influence policy, planning and program decisions. CDA policy also stipulates that the resident structure must have sufficient information about any program-related matter to be decided upon for a sufficient period of time so that it can initiate proposals and react intelligently.[4] How, then, did the residents on the one hand, and the CDA administrative staff on the other evaluate the flow of information with regards to important decisions and issues. A city was rated "good" on this variable if there was an established procedure for transmitting information to the residents and if the procedure insured that the residents had sufficient time to react to these issues intelligently. Rated "average" were those cities whose established procedure was not used consistently throughout the period under study. Cities were rated "poor" either if no procedure had been established or if an established procedure was not operationalized.

Var #18 ... <u>Extent and Nature of "Professional Cooperation" with Residents</u>

Planners' views on resident participation as a requirement in the planning process varies from frustration and discouragement to enthusiasm and advocacy. To what extent, then, did the professional planners and staff legitimately respond to the issues and concerns raised by residents?

Rated "strong" on Variable No. 18 were those cities in which the professional staff of the CDA (on loan to the CDA or assigned to the resident structure) were able to work out a viable working relationship with the residents, i.e., resident inputs were sought and integrated into the planning process, in an atmosphere of mutual respect and trust. Rated "general" were those in which the professional staff, as a whole, saw the residents role in the planned process as advisory and/or revisory, but not integral to the planning process. Rated "low" were those in which the professional staff, as a whole, saw the resident role in the planning process as antithetical to an "efficient" planning process, and thus proceeded with the planning process without integrating nor seeking to meaningfully integrate the inputs of the MNA residents.

Dependent Variables

The dependent variables are measures of resident control as manifested in the degree and extent of influence residents were able to exercise in the:

 ... hiring and firing of Model Cities personnel
 ... allocation of the Model Cities budget
 ... operation of Model Cities Programs
 ... initiation of Model Cities Programs

As such these variables (19-22) will be considered the criterion variables, i.e., variables by which the degrees of resident influence in the decision-making process in the Model Cities can be measured. These four decision-areas are essential to the consideration of control in most federal intervention programs which requires resident participation for its successful operation. In particular the demands of ghetto residents for community control of various municipal institutions and intervention programs have been clearly focused in these four areas: the right to have a say in who gets employed; how the money allocated to allegedly help the slum dwellers actually is disbursed; who runs and designs the programs for the slum dwellers. These questions underlined the concern of the have-nots for accountability of the programs and monies allocated to ameliorate the social and economic conditions which have and continue to oppress them. At best, most ethnic minority members believe that their influence in these decision areas will increase the potential of the intervention effort to succeed; at minimum their inputs in these areas are perceived as insurance that they will receive an equitable share of the side-effect benefits (jobs, building contracts, manpower training, "relevant" community programs, etc...) to be derived from a government program ostensibly promoted to improve their welfare.

OPERATIONALIZATION OF THE DEPENDENT VARIABLES

	DEPENDENT VARIABLES	DEGREE OF INFLUENCE
Var #19	Extent of Resident Influence in hiring and firing	1=Strong; 2=Shared; 3=Mild; 4=Low.
Var #20	Extent of Resident Influence in allocation of budget	1=Strong; 2=Shared; 3=Mild; 4=Low.
Var #21	Extent of Resident Influence in operation of programs	1=Strong; 2=Shared; 3=Mild; 4=Low.
Var #22	Extent of Resident Influence in initiation of programs	1=Strong; 2=Shared; 3=Mild; 4=Low.

Strong Influence - Each of the dependent variables was rated on an ordinal scale measuring the relative decision-influence residents were able to secure in these areas over the two year period under study. A city was rated strong if the MNA residents were able to exercise significant influence in most if not all of these four decision areas. In terms of Variable No. 19, for example, "strong" influence would mean that the local residents were able to serve a number of the Model Cities generated jobs for MNA residents, and were screened and selected by a committee which structure and composition reflected strong resident participation. Additionally, residents, through an established process, could influence the dismissal or question actions leading to the dismissal of a Model City employee.

Strong influence is characterized by a process established and mutually recognized by the resident structure and the CDA administrative office. The influence might be exercised through a legitimate contractual agreement, (e.g., a city ordinance between the city and the resident structure which has been passed and ratified by the council). The contractual agreement could be a formal

72

"de jure" authority specifying the roles of the resident structure in these decision-areas; or it could be contractual agreement which is less legally binding but perceived by both parties (resident structure and city) to be an obligatory agreement.

Shared Influence - Cities were rated shared influence if the residents were participants in most if not all of the decisions circumscribed by the criterion variables. Their influence is less than strong, in that their role in these areas were pro-forma, although these inputs were often considered and implemented. The critical difference between a rating of "strong" and that of "shared" is that in the latter resident influence impacted more on those decisions which were already made or in the making; i.e., residents were able to modify and at times even reverse decisions made without their inputs. Where the influence of those residents in cities rated strong was continuous and integral to the decisions made in these areas, the influence of residents in cities rated "shared" was exercised more at specific review or amendment junctures in these decision processes.

Mild Influence - A city was rated mild if the MNA residents were participants in some but not most of the decisions in these areas. Their influence is less than "strong" and "shared" in that there is no binding contractual agreement between them and the CDA specifying their roles, nor do they exercise particularly strong influence at particular junctures of the decision process. Although they participate, their roles are limited to advisory and revisionary activities within the acceptable bounds of the CDA. Furthermore, the intensity of their activities does not impact significantly on the ultimate decisions in these areas.

Low Influence - Rated low are those cities in which residents had minimum participation in these areas. Their participation, when it occurred was also limited to advisory and revisionary roles; and the intensity of their activity did not influence the ultimate decisions in these areas.

Rationale for Employing Ordinal Scales

An important aspect of this study approach is to be able to do a cross-city analysis of the results. This consideration was crucial in the decision to use eleven cities as the units of analysis, rather than one or two. The study is designed to maximize the comparability among the eleven cities and to allow for some generalization about resident participation in the Model

Cities Program as it affects the politics of ethnic minorities. The rating scales described in the previous section were employed to add a series of dimensions by which the cities could be described and easily compared. Although the ordinal categories and their associated values have a quantitative appearance, it should be noted that a city's rating on these scales were made by a single individual scrutinizing the chronologies of each city. Consequently, the ratings reflect the accuracy of this scrutiny based on the rationales previously defined, in much the same way as they do the accuracy of the MKGK chronologies. Among the many practical advantages cited in favor of a rating approach are the fact that it takes less time, it can be used with a large number of subjects and variables, and works well even with relatively untrained raters.[5] The major objection of the rating approach is the potential error or question of reliability of ratings based only on broad impressions about the subject being rated. This objection is not a significant limitation to this study, however, since the chronologies are fairly objective reports of the events and issues as they occurred in each city. To the extent that this objection considers the broad impressionistic judgements of poorly defined traits especially when recorded after the observations were made, the validity of the chronologies is fairly high. As previously noted, MKGK maintained a staff which constantly monitored the events as they occurred, thus insuring an accurate report of the event. In order to compensate for the possible errors which might have occurred due to a single judgement procedure, the ranking procedure employed required only that the cities rated be placed in order to each trait (variable) used. Thus, for example, a city's rating on the "sympathy of the CDA Director for the Issues of Community Control" divided the cities between those with strong CDC support, mild support, and the low support. This approach gives the rater considerable latitude over the trait being rated and lessens the possibility (as when the categories were more discretely graded) of error. This ranking approach is considered most desirable when a single rater is to rate the whole group of subjects.[6]

The ordinal scales employed in this study effort, then, serve several purposes. Their primary utility is a quantification technique which allows a standardized response mode and provides data on the variables related to the study. In addition, the scales serve as a data reduction technique, reducing the data of the chronologies relevant to the present study to a finite number of variables. Finally, since the scales are ordinal in nature, they lend themselves to more sophisticated analytic techniques, than would merely nominal scales.

General Analytic Procedures

After the set of quantitative data had been gathered and operationalized, empirical investigation could begin. The general focus of the study is: Has "widespread citizen participation," enhanced the political efficiency; i.e., increased control over the institutions and decision-making processes that affect ethnic minorities. Within the parameters of this study, the operational questions are: First, can measures of participation (independent variables) make it possible to predict increased control (dependent variables)? And additionally, what impact do the intervening variables have on the relationship between the independent and dependent variables? It was anticipated that the higher the intensity of resident participation, the greater would be the degree of resident control. In keeping with the more usual model in social sciences, the overall null hypothesis to be tested is: there is no relationship between participation and control.

Basically, two analytic procedures were used to test the null hypothesis. Both employed the use of computer technology to compute the Goodman and Kruskal coefficient of ordinal association and the Pearsons coefficient of correlation.

The Goodman and Kruskal Coefficient, generally known as "gamma", is the most commonly used ordinal measure of association. Its underlying logic is basically simple, and its procedure easily employed. Essentially, the degree of association between the scales being measured is estimated by the degree to which the subject's relative rating on one ordinal scale is predictable from its rating on another. As can be discerned, this analytic tool is readily applicable to the problem of analysis at hand. For example, a city's rating on "CDA director sympathy with community control," could be measured against the city's rating on "population size;" "type of municipal government;" "information flow from the CDA to the resident structure;" or any other ordinal scale on which the city was rated. The highest possible association is attained when a city's rating is in exactly the same order or exactly the opposite order on any two scales.

In both of these cases, perfect agreement and perfect inversion, we can guess a city's rank on one of these scales from its rank on the other. In general then, to determine the degree of association or predictability between two ordinal scales, one has to examine the degree to which they tend either toward agreement or inversion in order.

The strength of association between the criterion variables (measuring control; Variables Nos. 19-22) and the independent and intervening variables, would give us an estimate of which variable(s) is the most powerful predictor of the extent of decision-making influence residents attained in their respective localities. In order to test the strength of association with the Goodman-Kruskal procedure, the four criterion variables were summated on a single scale measuring the cumulative resident influence attained. Essentially, then, a new variable or scale was constructed. The gamma coefficient was then estimated for the association between the criterion variable scale and all other variables (1-18) identified in the study.

To compute the relationship between the dependent variables as a whole and the independent and intervening variables as a whole, an additional analytic procedure was employed. The Likert Scaling Program, a computerized scaling technique, was employed to compute:

1. The degree of association between the variables constituting the respective sets of dependent, independent and intervening variables; i.e., what is the extent of inter-correlation among the respective sets of variables? How well do they "hang" together? To what extent does a city rating on one scale allow us to predict his score on another scale in the same set?

2. The degree of association or predictability between the dependent variables, summated on a single scale, on the one hand and the independent and intervening variables, also summated on a single interval scale, on the other.

In summary, a thorough examination of the literature and the chronologies revealed that a number of factors seemed to have an impact on the degree and extent of decision influence residents were able to exercise in a local Model Cities Program. Those variables which were consistently apparent and quantifiable across the eleven cities (as repeated in the chronologies) were identified and classified as:

   ... <u>Intervening Variables</u> - those which characterized the socio-political character of the city and the Model Neighborhood residents as a whole.

... <u>Independent Variables</u> - those which measured the actual participation, or the pre-conditions for the effective participation of the local residents.

... <u>Dependent Variables</u> - those which measured the actual decision influence of the local residents in the program's operation.

Each of these variables constitutes one characteristic of a particular Model Cities Program. As a whole, they allow us to view the Model Cities Program as a set of variables introduced into an existing set of relationships that constitutes an urban system. Change in one aspect of the urban system should produce changes in other aspects of the system. Hypothetically, the introduction of the Model Cities Program should produce a complex set of adjustments between the various elements within the system which should allow previously deprived residents in the urban system to be included as a result of the adjustment.

To test the overall null hypothesis of this study two analytic procedures were used, the first is a non-parametric technique of computing the strength of association between two ordinal scales; the other is parametric and was used to test the strength of association between the collective sets of intervening and independent variables against the criterion variables.

Footnotes - Chapter IV:

1. Model Cities funding allowed City Demonstration Agencies one year of planning. During the second year, program activities planned during the first
   year were operationalized.

2. Edward C. Banfield's reader, Urban Government - Chapter IV - provides
   interesting reading on this subject. As a whole, Banfield argues that the
   non-partisan election system and the manager-council form of municipal
   government are associated with a strong, independent executive who will
   ignore special interest and assert his "impartial" conception of the
   interest of the "community as a whole".

3. Technical Assistance Bulletin #1, "Appropriate Uses of Model Cities Planning
   Grants Funds, and Model Cities Staffing", MCGR G 3110.1 November, 1967,
   Paragraph 3.a.

4. CDA Letter #3.

5. G. C. Helmstader, Research Concepts in Human Behavior, Meredith Corporation,
   New York, 1970, p. 362.

6. G. C. Helmstader, op. cit. for a discussion on the uses of rating scales,
   and the appropriateness of the "ranking procedure".

CHAPTER V

STUDY FINDINGS

Introduction

It is appropriate to recapitulate briefly the questions to be examined.
The major concern is the consideration of the process of "widespread citizen
participation" as it has been operationalized in eleven American cities. Of
particular interest are the conditions under which ethnic minorities in the target areas of the Model Cities Program were able to exercise decision-influence
through the participation process which evolved in each locality.

Operationally, "resident participation" was defined as those activities
undertaken by MNA residents to influence the program and its resources to meet
their self-perceived needs. Inherent in this definition is a recognition that
the style and extent of the residents' activities are contingent on many factors
in the Model Cities action arena. Through a thorough examination of the literature on resident participation and the MKGK chronologies, many of these factors
(variables) have been identified. Among others they include: the extent to
which residents played a part in the application for a Model Cities grant; the
extent to which they played a part in the selection of the CDA director and the
extent to which they played a role in designing and developing the resident participation structure itself. These factors (variables) within the methodological
framework used in this research effort, represent the variables by which the
residents' actual involvement in the Model Cities decision-making activities can
be measured. Essentially,they index the actual involvement of residents in the
significant decisions and program activities observable within the scope of the
chronologies.

In addition to these variables of actual involvement, the literature
and the chronologies suggest that other factors, though less concrete (and more
difficult to measure) also affect the "intensity of resident activity". These
factors are the general will of the residents themselves to become involved in
the Model Cities process; the encouragement on the part of city officials and
Model Cities administrators to stimulate resident activity; and the extent of
ancillary services (technical assistance) provided to facilitate MNA residents'
participation in program activities and decisions. Several variables have been
identified in this research effort which approximate the extent to which these

factors affected the intensity of resident participation. They include the extent of community cohesiveness generated by the Model Cities process; CDA director's sympathy with the issues of community control; the extent of the Model Cities professional staffs' cooperation with the residents, and the information flow from the CDA to the resident structure.

Lastly, the environment in which the Model Cities process is operationalized, is also thought to host factors which might affect the "intensity of resident activity". These include the local governmental type of political organization (city manager, strong-mayor, etc.), the racial composition of the city, and the extent of racial disturbances (if any) which occurred in the city previous and during the Model Cities program.

Theoretically, it is assumed that all of the factors identified have an affect on the "intensity of resident participation" and thus on the degree of influence or control residents are able to exercise in the Model Cities program. In this respect the extent of the resident influence in the hiring/firing of Model Cities personnel, in the allocation of the Model Cities budget resources, in the operation and initiation of programs can be seen as outcome measures of the "intensity of resident activity". (See Chart 1).

Operationally, though, the research question is: can measures of participation make it possible to predict the degree of influence residents were able to exercise in the Model Cities program? In addition, what effect do environmental factors have on the degree of influence gained by residents? Following the theoretical assumptions stated previously, it is anticipated that the higher the intensity of resident activity the higher the degree of resident control. It will be recalled that in order to pursue an analysis of the research question, the factors previously identified as having an effect on the "intensity of resident activity were classified into: Independent, intervening and dependent variables. They were then operationalized in accordance to rating scales. These scales ordinal in nature, rated the variables from most to least in having the relevant attribute consistent with effective resident participation.

The analytic procedures used were facilitated by the use of the Data-Text Computer programs and a Likert Scaling program designed by Dr. Kenneth Jones. With Data-Text the degree of association between the independent and the dependent variables and the intervening and the dependent variables was computed. Additionally, to determine the overall impact of the collective set of independent and intervening variables respectively on the dependent variables, the

CHART 1

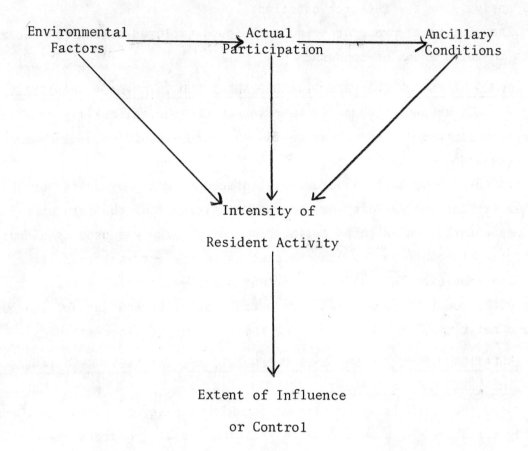

Likert Scaling program was used to compute the degree of association between the independent variables summated and measured on a single scale. A similar procedure was used to test the degree of association between the intervening and dependent variables.

A crucial part of this study was the development of a set of criteria by which the variables were rated on ordinal scales. The scaling of each variable provided the source data for the empirical analysis of the research question. The results of the ratings, shown on Table #1, represent the first step in reducing the information from the chronologies to a set of quantifiable data. Once this data was obtained it was then possible to proceed with an empirical analysis of the research question.

The analytical procedures and techniques employed essentially address themselves to three areas of concern:

1.   COHESIVENESS OF THE SETS OF INDEPENDENT AND INTERVENING VARIABLES

In this area an attempt is made to compute the reliability coefficient (alpha) of the clustered sets of variables that were classified as independent, intervening and dependent.

To the extent that the clustering procedure was judgemental no hard evidence exists for the validity or internal consistency of the sets of variables. Consequently, the Likert Scaling computer program was used as a confirmatory analytic procedure to provide evidence as to the internal consistency of the sets of variables. This was an important step, especially in regard to the variables which constituted measures of control, or criterion variables, against which the other variables were tested for their degree of association.

2.   RELATIONSHIP OF THE SET OF INDEPENDENT, AND INTERVENING VARIABLES TO THE DEPENDENT VARIABLES

Here the focus is on the extent to which the set of independent and intervening variables, each summed on an individual scale, correlate with the dependent variables, also summed on an individual scale. In other words, what are the scale to scale correlations of the sets of independent, intervening and dependent variables when each set is summed on a single scale. Again the Likert Scaling program technique facilitated this procedure.

3.   RELATIONSHIP OF EACH OF THE INDEPENDENT AND INTERVENING VARIABLES TO A SINGLE SUMMED MEASURE OF CONTROL - THE DEPENDENT VARIABLES

The specific concern of this phase of the analysis is the measure of association between the dependent variables, and the other variables. Here the dependent variables are summed to obtain a single value measuring the decision influence of the residents in the program. Each of the variables identified in the study are then measured against the criterion variable (measuring control) to obtain the degree of association.

Cities / Variables	C A M B	A T L A	D A Y T	D E N V	D E T R	G A R Y	R E A D	R O C H	P I T T	R I C H	S A N T	Key to Rating Scales
Var 1 Size of City	3	1	2	2	1	2	3	2	1	3	1	1=Lg(Above 325000) 2=Med(150,000-325,000) 3=Sm(150,000)
Var 2 Type of Municipal Government	1	3	1	3	3	3	2	1	3	1	2	1=City Mgr 2=Comm or Weak Mayor-Strong Council 3=Strong Mayor
Var 3 Race & Ethnic Composition of City	3	1	2	2	2	1	3	2	2	2	1	1=Lg(Above 30%) 2=Med (Between 15-30%) 3=Sm(Below 15%)
Var 4 Race & Ethnic Composition of MNA	3	1	1	1	2	1	3	2	2	2	1	1=Lg(Above 30%) 2=Med (Between 20-60%) 3=Sm(Below 20%)
Var 5 Indices of Racial Conflict in City/MNA-Prior to M.C.	3	2	1	3	3	3	2	1	3	3	3	1=Major Conflict 2=Med Conflict 3=Small Conflict
Var 6 Indices of Racial Conflict in City/MNA-During M.C.	2	2	1	2	1	3	2	3	1	2	3	1=Major Conflict 2=Med Conflict 3=Small Conflict
Var 7 Comm Organiz Cohesiveness Gen by M.C.Activ.	1	3	1	3	2	3	3	1	2	2	2	1=Very Cohesive 2=Gen Cohesive 3=Minimally Cohesive
Var 8 Resident Involvement in M.C. Application	2	3	2	3	2	3	2	3	3	1	3	1=Very Active Involvement 2=Mild Involvement 3=No Involvement
Var 9 Indices of Res Activ. for Increased Roles in M.C. Process	1	3	1	2	2	3	2	1	1	3	3	1=Strong/Insistent 2-Strong 3=Mild
Var 10 Res Participa in Selection of M.C. Director	1	2	1	2	2	2	2	2	2	1	2	1=Influence 2=No Influence
Var 11 Represent. of Resident Structure of Neighborhd.	1	4	1	3	3	2	4	2	4	2	3	1=Very Represent 2=Generally 3=Minimally 4=Not representative
Var 12 Directors Sympathy with Community Control	1	3	1	2	3	3	3	2	2	1	3	1=Strong Support 2=Mild Support 3=No Support
Var 13 Role of Resid. in Establishing Prerogatives of "CDA-MC Structure"	1	4	1	2	2	3	2	2	3	4	3	1=Dominant Role-2=Active Role 3=Mild Role 4=No Role
Var 14 Structure of C.P. Body	2	2	1	2	1	2	2	1	1	2	2	1=Separate C.P. Structure 2=Within the CDA
Var 15 Role of Resid. in Estab. Prerog. of the C.P.Body	1	3	1	2	2	3	2	1	3	2	2	1=Strong Role 2=Active Role 3=Mild Role
Var 16 % of Ethnic Minority in on the C.P. Body	3	2	1	1	1	1	3	1	2	1	1	1=Dominant(60%or Greater)2=Equity (Bet 40-60%) 3=Inequity (Below 40%)
Var 17 Information Flow From CDA to Resident Body	1	3	1	2	2	3	2	2	3	1	2	1=Good 2=Average 3=Poor
Var 18 Extent of Professional Cooperation w/Residents	2	3	1	3	2	3	2	3	3	1	3	1=Strong 2=General 3=Low
Var 19 Extent of Resid. Influ. in Hiring/Firing M.C. Personnel	1	4	1	3	2	3	4	2	3	2	4	1=Strong 2=Shared 3=Mild 4=Low
Var 20 Extent of Resid. Influ. in Alloc of Budg.Resour.	1	4	1	3	2	3	4	2	3	3	4	1=Strong 2=Shared 3=Mild 4=Low
Var 21 Extent of Resid Influ. in Opr of M.C.Programs	2	4	1	4	3	4	3	2	4	3	4	1=Strong 2=Shared 3=Mild 4=Low
Var 22 Extent of Resi. Influ. in Initiation of Prog.	1	4	1	3	3	3	3	2	3	2	3	1=Strong 2=Shared 3=Mild 4=Low

Chart 2

Intervening Variables	Independent Variables	Intervening Variables
Environment - I	Measures of Participation	Environment - II

Environment - I

1. Size of City

2. Ethnic Composition of City

3. Type of Municipal Government

4. Race and Ethnic Composition of MNA

Measures of Participation

1. Resident Involvement in Application Period

2. Resident Activity for Increased Role in M.C. Process

3. Representativeness of Resident Structure

4. Directors Sympathy with Community Control

5. Role of Residents in Designing "MC-CDA" Structure

6. Structure of Resident Body

7. Role of Residents in Establishing

8. % Ethnic Minorities on C.P. Structure

9. Information - Flow

10. Professional Cooperation with Residents

Environment - II

1. Racial Conflict Prior to M.C.

2. Racial Conflict During M.C.

3. Organizational Cohesiveness of Residents

Dependent Variables

Measures of Control

1. Extent of Resident Influence in Hiring/Firing

2. Extent of Resident Influence in Allocation of Budget

3. Extent of Resident Influence in Operation of Programs

4. Extent of Resident Influence in Initiation of Programs

Significance Levels

In this chapter the detailed results of the empirical analysis of the data will be presented. In the following discussions, correlations will be emphasized at their reported level of significance. It must be noted, however, that the sampling procedure employed to select the eleven cities was not a random sampling of the universe of the existing one-hundred and fifty (150) Model Cities programs. As pointed out previously, the eleven city sample was selected jointly by the HUD and MKGK staff with a deliberate aim of insuring their representativeness of the universe. The process of sample selection was successful in pooling a set of Model Cities programs, which, within the expertise of both HUD and MKGK staff, enhanced the generalizability of their study findings. The implications and generalizations which might be inferred from the level of significance of the correlations reported in this chapter, then, is conditioned by the sampling procedure used by the MKGK and HUD staff. The important focus of analysis in study does not rest wholly on its power of generalization, but also on the strength of associations observed throughout the chronologies. In respect to the latter focus, the test of significance assumes less importance since the eleven city sample is the universe.

Study Findings

1. COHESIVENESS OF THE SETS OF INDEPENDENT, INTERVENING AND DEPENDENT VARIABLES

   A. Dependent Variables - Measures of Control

ITEM CORRELATION MATRIX	Var # 19	Var # 20	Var # 21	Var # 22
Var #19 Extent of resident influences in hiring/ firing of Model Cities staff		.96	.83	.88
Var #20 Extent of resident influence in allocation of budget resources			.84	.84
Var #21 Extent of Resident influence in operation of Model Cities program				.90
Var #22 Extent of resident influence in initiation of programs				

As the above table shows, each of the variables measuring control has a very high correlation with the other variables. The computed correlation is significant for an N of eleven cities at the .05 level of significance.[1]

Additionally, the reliability coefficient (alpha) of this set of variables is very high at .963. These statistics support the original logic of clustering these four variables. More importantly it provides evidence that if the score (or rating) of any one of the four variables is known, the score (or rating) of the other 3 variables could be predicted with a high degree of accuracy. Thus, for example, if a city was rated high on variable 19, we could expect that the city would also be rated high on variables 20, 21, and 22.

These findings suggest that the degree of influence residents were able to exercise in any of one of the four areas of control, provided a good indication of the extent of influence in the other 3 areas. It was unlikely to find the residents of a city having strong influence on one of the four variables measuring control and low influence in any one of the other 3 areas. It would seem that if the intensity of resident activities was such that it lead residents to extend significant influence in one area, everything else being equal, the momentum of the intensity would carry over to increase their influence in the other areas of control.

B. Intervening Variables - Environment - I

ITEM CORRELATION MATRIX		Var # 1	Var # 2	Var # 3	Var # 4
Var #1	Size of the city		⁻.55	.55	.49
Var #2	Type of municipal government			⁻.44	⁻.37
Var #3	Race and ethnic composition of city				.86
Var #4	Race and ethnic composition of MNA				

Using the .05 level of significance, the item correlation matrix as a whole does not appear to be significant. The exception is the correlation between variables #3 and #4. Here, as we would expect, there is a significant correlation between the population of ethnic minorities in the city as a whole with that of the Model Neighborhood Area. In this regard we could say that the Model Cities program did indeed concentrate operations in those blighted areas of the city where the greater number of ethnic minorities resided. In other words, if a city had a large ethnic minority population, we could expect that the designated area for the Model City operations would contain a large ethnic minority population.

The more interesting aspects of these findings, though, are the directions of association among this set of variables. There is an inverse relationship between city size and type of municipal government, as well as between type of municipal government and ethnic composition of the City/MNA. These inverse relationships suggest: A) that the larger the city the more likely its government would be structured around a "strong-mayor" type of government and vice-versa; B) the larger the ethnic population of the city the more likely the governmental structure would be the "strong-mayor" type of government.

What is important though, is that certain city governmental structures might have a constraining effect on the attainment of increased influence in decision-making by ethnic minorities.

The reliability coefficient (alpha) for this set of variables was low at .103. Alpha is a statistic measuring the extent to which a set of variables vary in the same direction. More explicitly, it gives the mean of the correlations resulting from all possible ways of splitting a given test (or scales) into two halves.[2] As noted, three of the six item intercorrelations in this cluster, represent inverse relationships, thus affecting the overall computation of alpha.

C. Intervening Variables - Environment - II

ITEM CORRELATION MATRIX	Var # 5	Var # 6	Var # 7
Var #5 Racial conflict prior to Model Cities		.0	.37
Var #6 Racial conflict during Model Cities			.16
Var #7 Organizational cohesiveness generated by Model Cities			

Racial conflicts in one time period are not good predictors of future conflicts. Other factors must be taken into consideration. A list of these might include more definitive economic and social descriptive statistics of the city's disadvantaged population at the time a conflict occurred (assuming, of course, that the conflict is engendered by the "have-nots" social and economic conditions) in relation to the same factors in a different time period. Other factors, though less tangible and difficult to measure - like the extent of racist attitudes or hostility among the general city population - might be additional important factors. However, the statistical procedures employed in this study did not address themselves to these issues. In any event, racial conflicts might be seen as the cathartic product of social and economic frustrations. As such it would be the conditions which might be the important factorial predictors of future conflicts, and not the conflict in and of itself.

The assumption that members of the ethnic minority population are more likely to be organizationally cohesive in the aftermath of racial conflicts is slightly supported. In addition it appears that those cities which experienced racial conflict prior to Model Cities were more organizationally cohesive than those experiencing racial conflict during the program's operation.

The rationale for clustering this set of variables is not strongly supported by these correlation coefficients. The reliability coefficient was computed at .398.

ITEM CORRELATION MATRIX		Var # 8	Var # 9	Var # 10	Var # 11	Var # 12	Var # 13	Var # 14	Var # 15	Var # 16	Var # 17	Var # 18
Var #8	Resident involvement in Model Cities application		.0	.74	.37	.51	.10	.05	.38	-.13	.75	.93
Var #9	Indices of resident activity for increase role in M.C. process			.24	.30	.51	.76	.66	.58	-.27	.29	.14
Var #10	Resident participation in the section of M.C. director(s)				.75	.87	.28	.04	.55	-.09	.83	.82
Var #11	Representativeness of resident structure of the Neighborhood constituency					.69	.50	.10	.69	.24	.69	.49
Var #12	Director's sympathy with community control						.34	.16	.59	-.01	.74	.60
Var #13	Role of residents in establishing the prerogatives of the "CDA-M.C." structure							.35	.75	-.20	.50	.26
Var #14	Structure of the resident participation body								.26	.29	.0	.11
Var #15	Role of residents in establishing the prerogatives of the resident participation body									.0	.83	.48
Var #16	Percentage of ethnic minority on citizen participation body										.0	-.03
Var #17	Information flow from CDA to resident body											.80
Var #18	Extent of professional cooperation with residents											

The variables in this matrix represent the actual involvement and the pre-conditions for effective participation of residents in the Model Cities process. As a set these variables had a very high reliability coefficient of .865, suggesting strong internal consistency. Both the dependent variables measuring control and the independent variables measuring participation had considerable internal consistency; i.e., they hung together well. They were in effect good cross predictors of each other.

At the .602 level of significance, var #8 (resident involvement in the M. C. application) is significantly correlated with var #18, #17 and #10. The extent of the resident participation in the application period could be seen as a critical factor for setting the stage for effective participation. In fact, the extent of resident participation in the crucial initiatory steps of the program determined the degree of cooperation to be attained from the professionals (largely drawn from the cities line agencies) and whether the residents would have an influential voice (or any at all) in the selection of the CDA director.

Var #9 "Indices of resident activity for an increased role in the Model Cities process" is significantly associated with var #14, and #13. The relative satisfaction of the residents with their established roles varied directly with the organizational location of the resident participation structure. Resident structures which were outside the organizational hegemony of the CDA tended to engage in more deliberate actions to increase their overall influence in the programs.

Var #10 was assumed to be one of the more important determinants of effective resident participation. This variable is significantly associated with var #18, #17, #12, and #11. As previously noted, the CDA director plays an important role in the Model Cities process, particularly in terms of resident participation. These findings largely underscore this importance.

The residents' role in the selection of the director varied with the representativeness of the elected (or selected) resident participation group. If and when residents did participate in the selection of the director (of the eleven cities only three had any influence in the selection and appointment of the director, while in the other cities the director was expressly appointed by the municipal chief), they tended to support a candidate who demonstrated sympathy with the issues of community control. Other positive benefits seem to flow from the resident participation of the director. Information necessary for the inter-communication between residents and the CDA and the extent of professional cooperation -- both pre-conditions necessary for effective participation -- were significantly associated with var #10. These associations suggest that where residents were able to influence the selection of the director, other factors favorable to effective resident participation was enhanced.

Var #11 -- <u>Representativeness of the resident structure of the neighbor-hood constituency</u> -- is significantly associated with var #17, #15, and #12. When realized, representative resident structures were largely reflective of the local Model Cities administrators and staff's early and earnest attempts to stimulate the attention of the total community in the resident representatives elections. The CDA director, sympathetic to community control through effective resident partici-pation, dedicated a significant amount of time and energy to attract the participa-tion of the total community in the resident elections.

Var #12 -- <u>Director's sympathy with community control</u> -- is significantly associated with var #17 and #18. As previously noted, several benefits of resident participation are enhanced if the CDA director is sympathetic with strong resident input in the program operation. These findings indicate that such a CDA director insured that the residents obtained the necessary professional cooperation and information needed for effective participation.

Var #13 -- <u>Role of residents in establishing the prerogatives of the CDA structure</u> is significantly associated with var #15. Here the implication is straightforward. Simply put, residents who participated in the ground rule affect-ing the decision roles and areas of the CDA office also had some input in estab-lishing their own decision roles and prerogatives.

Var #15 -- <u>Role of residents in establishing the prerogatives of the resident participation body</u> -- is significantly correlated with Var #17. This finding again suggests that once the ground rules, rights and responsibilities of the residents were settled the communication between both structures was continuous, or at least not arbitrarily aborted at important decision junctures.

Var #16 -- <u>Percentage of ethnic minority on the resident participation structure</u> -- is not significantly associated with any of the other variables mea-suring participation. The intensity of resident participation is not influenced by the ethnic composition of the resident structure.

Var #17 -- <u>Information flow from CDA to resident body</u> -- is significantly associated with extent of professional cooperation with residents, a finding that speaks for itself.

In summary, the most significant variables influencing the intensity of resident participation are:

Var #10 - <u>Resident participation in the selection of the CDA director</u>

Var #11 - <u>Representativeness of the residence structure of the</u>

neighborhood constituency

Var #12 - CDA Director's sympathy with community control

Var #15 - Roles of residents in establishing the prerogatives of the resident participation structure

Var #17 - Information flow from CDA to resident body

These variables accounted for most of the variations in this sub-set, each having a Pearsonian coefficient of .80 or above when correlated to the summated value (scale) of all other variables in the subset.

The set of variables constituting the dependent variables (measures of control) and the set constituting the independent variables (measure of participation) show a high degree of internal consistency. The computed alpha coefficient in each case was significantly high, thus verifying the assumptions and rationale employed to cluster these sets of variables.

The computational analysis of alpha for Environmental I suggests on the one hand that "city size", "type of municipal structure", "race and ethnic composition of the city" and "race and ethnic composition" of the MNA are independent events. On the other hand, from a careful observation of these variables from Table #1, the notion that the size of the city and the size of the ethnic population of the city are not related does not appear to be that clear cut. Nor does the suggestion that "type of city government" and size of population are completely independent events seem entirely justifiable from an examination of Table #1. Given these observations, the effect of inverse relationships on the computation of alpha needs to be considered.

The computed alpha for Environmental II did not strongly support the clustering of these variables. This finding suggests that the probability of predicting the organizational cohesiveness likely to be generated by model city activity given knowledge of either a racial conflict prior or during model cities is not very high.

In terms of the inter-correlations of the respective sets of variables, several noticeable patterns appear to be important.

    A.   There is a "spill over" effect in the acquisition of significant influence in the programs' operation as measured by the dependent variables. If residents gain significant influence in one area of control, they are likely to gain significant influence in the others.

    B.   Large cities tend to have large ethnic minority populations, large ethnic populations in the MNA, and to be governed by "strong-mayor" governmental structures.

C. Cities which experience racial conflicts prior to Model Cities tend to have a more organizationally cohesive MNA than those which experienced racial conflict during the program.

D. MNA residents who participated in the early planning stages of the Model Cities program, that is, the application period, were able to develop positively reinforcing relationships with the professional staff of the program. This trend suggests that when residents were significantly involved in the early planning periods they were able to clear the path to effective participation of contentious "power-issues", thus securing relatively reinforcing relationships with the Model Cities staff.

E. The relative organizational cohesiveness of the Model Neighborhood area enhances several determinants of residents' potential influence in the program. Organizationally cohesive MNAs tended to secure significant inputs in the selection of the CDA director, and the roles their community organizations played in the Model Cities program relative to that of the CDA.
Furthermore, such MNAs supported the selection of CDA director candidates who were most sympathetic to community control through strong participation. Once such an endorsement was established the continuing participation of residents in the program was facilitated, that is, professionals tended to be more cooperative and information flowed more smoothly between the resident structure and the CDA.

2. RELATIONSHIP OF THE SET OF INDEPENDENT AND INTERVENING VARIABLES TO THE DEPENDENT VARIABLES

In this phase of the data analysis, each of the sub-sets of variables constituting the independent, dependent and intervening variables are summated on a single interval scale. The scales are then correlated with each other to determine the strength of association between them. The following table summarizes the results of this computational analysis.

SCALE TO SCALE CORRELATIONS	1	2	3	4
1 Dependent Variables - Measure of Control		⁻59	.73	.95
2 Intervening Variables - Environment - I			⁻36	⁻61
3 Intervening Variables - Environment - II				.72
4 Independent Variables - Measure of Participation				

The findings of the above scale do not support the overall null hypothesis of this study. The Pearsonian coefficient of correlation between the collective impact of the variables measuring participation and those measuring control is highly significant (.95). There is a significant and positive relationship between the intensity of resident participation and the extent of resident control.

There is also a significant and positive association between the extent of resident decision-influence in the Model Cities program and the collective impact of racial disturbances both prior and during the programs operation and the extent of organizational cohesiveness in the Model Neighborhood area (.72). On the other hand, there is a significant inverse relationship between resident control and the collective impact of the size of the city, its ethnic population, that of its MNA, and its governmental structure.[3] This finding suggests in general that residents in large cities with large ethnic minority populations are likely to have less decision-influence in the Model Cities program.

The collective impact of "Environment I", or the intervening variables measuring city size, type of municipal government, and the race and composition of the city and the MNA, on the intensity of participation is significantly negative; i.e., there is an inverse relationship between Environmental I and the intensity of participation. Large cities with large ethnic minority populations tend to have low resident participation in their model cities program.

On the other hand there is a significant and positive relationship between the collective impact of "Environment II" - the intervening variables measuring the extent of racial disturbances both prior and during model cities - and the intensity of participation. The greater the extent of racial disturbances prior and during Model Cities and the greater the community organization cohesiveness, the greater will be the intensity of resident participation.

In sum, the intensity of resident participation varies directly with the extent of resident influence in the:

1. hiring and firing of Model Cities personnel
2. the allocation of Model Cities budget resources
3. the initiation of programs
4. the operation of programs

The two sets of intervening variables impact significantly on both the intensity of resident participation and the level of resident control. In general, large cities with large ethnic minority populations tend to host residents who gain less decision-influence due to less intense participation.

The trend which emerges from the analysis of the data is that ethnic minority residents in large urban cities are less likely to gain significant influence in the Model Cities program. Later in the study more detailed discussion of this trend will be developed in light of other significant associations presented in this chapter. Having established, however, that there is a positive and significant association between the independent and dependent variables, which variables are the most powerful predictors of resident control?

The following table presents the Goodman-Kruskal (Gamma) coefficient of ordinal association between each of the variables identified in the study and the criterion variables summated on a single scale. It will be remembered that the gamma coefficient is an indicator of the relative probability of predicting a city's rating on one scale (variable) knowing its score on another. In this regard, to what extent does a city rating on each or any of the variables identified in the study allow us to predict the relative decision-influence residents would exercise in a Model Cities program?

The gamma coefficient could be seen as the relative weight or strength of a variable to predict the relative influence residents might exercise in a Model Cities program.

3. <u>RELATIONSHIP OF EACH OF THE INDEPENDENT AND INTERVENING VARIABLES</u>
<u>TO A SINGLE SUMMATED MEASURE OF CONTROL</u>

VARIABLES	GAMMA
Size of City	-.250
Type of Municipal Government	.429
Race and Ethnic Composition of City	.500
Race and Ethnic Composition of MNA	-.185
Indices of Racial Conflict Prior to Model Cities	-.083
Indices of Racial Conflict During Model Cities	.500
Community Cohesiveness Generated by Model Cities Activity	.852
Resident Involvement in Model Cities Application	.478
Indices of Resident Activity for Increased Role in M.C. Process	.846
Resident Participation in Selection of M.C. Director	1.000*
Representativeness of Resident Structure of the M.N.A.	.923
Directors Sympathy with Community Control	1.000*
Role of Residents in Establishing the Prerogatives of the CDA Structure	.775
Structure of C.P. Body	.667
Role of Residents in Establishing the Prerogatives of the Resident Participation Structure	.692
Percentage of Ethnic Minority on Resident Participation Structure	.124
Information Flow from CDA to Resident Participation	.446
Extent of Professional Cooperation with Residents	.583

---

*These ordinal coefficients suggest that this is perfect congruence between these variables and the summated value of the criterion variables. They are unusually high, however, since both variables were originally scaled on a dichotomous item scale; i.e., "influence or no influence" and "sympathy or no sympathy", and since the criterion variables were also summated on a single scale and also dichotomous in nature; i.e., "control or no control". In computing the ordinal association between two dichotomous scales, it is not unusual to get a perfect coefficient of either congruence or inversion.

The table of significance of gamma with an N of eleven (11) indicate the critical (significant) level to be .491. The following variables, then, are listed in order of their relative predictive strength of resident control.

... CDA DIRECTOR'S SYMPATHY WITH COMMUNITY CONTROL

... RESIDENT PARTICIPATION IN SELECTION OF THE CDA DIRECTOR

... REPRESENTATIVENESS OF THE RESIDENT STRUCTURE OF THE MODEL NEIGHBORHOOD

... COMMUNITY COHESIVENESS GENERATED BY MODEL CITIES ACTIVITY

... INDICES OF RESIDENT ACTIVITY FOR AN INCREASED ROLE IN THE MODEL CITIES PROCESS

... ROLE OF RESIDENTS IN ESTABLISHING THE PREROGATIVES OF THE CDA STRUCTURE

... ROLE OF RESIDENTS IN ESTABLISHING THE PREROGATIVES OF THE RESIDENT PARTICIPATION STRUCTURE

... STRUCTURE OF THE C.P. BODY (ORGANIZATIONAL LOCATION)

... EXTENT OF PROFESSIONAL COOPERATION WITH RESIDENTS

... INDICES OF RACIAL CONFLICT DURING MODEL CITIES

... RACE AND ETHNIC COMPOSITION OF CITY

Theoretically, these variables prescribe the conditions under which maximum resident participation was attained by MNA residents. They allow us to sketch a scenario of activities which must be promoted on the part of residents, encouraged by the CDA director, and sanctioned by the city itself. As operational conditions for resident participation, they can be divided into the following categories:

A. Resident Activities - The MNA should have community organizations working cooperatively previous to, or at least in regards to, the Model Cities Program. The manifest cohesiveness of the community organizations must be reflected in the structure and composition of the elected or appointed resident participation body. The resident structure should be separate from the administrative hegemony on the CDA office. Residents must at all times energetically seek to resolve those issues which could potentially ameliorate their prerogatives in the program's operation.

B. CDA Director's Activities - In addition to his general administrative competence, the CDA director should be oriented toward a resident advocacy orientation. This orientation should be manifested in administrative practices which allow the residents to be real participants in the decision areas of the program's operation. Moreover, the CDA director should use the ability and willingness to work with the MNA residents in the planning process as an essential criterion for hiring professional staff.

C. City's Influence - The municipal authorities should recognize that the development of a strong resident participation component is integral to the program's success. This recognition should be manifested at least by insuring that residents have a definitive and substantive role in the application phase of the programs and in the selection of the CDA director.

Contextual Summary of the Research Findings

The findings from the empirical analysis are summarized here, with specific regard to areas out of which answers to the major questions of this study can come. It must be kept clear that because of the limitations inherent in this study, the generalizability of the findings are subject to common sense appraisal as well as further empirical validation. Moreover, current and past research and analysis by other students of the participation issue should provide some grounding as to the generalizability of the findings. The findings do, however, have credibility that is not ordinarily derived from typical survey research. The unique contribution of this study is the use of complete chronologies of events (case studies) gathered by trained, objective observers which in turn could be coded and translated into quantitative measures via rating scales so that these narrative reports could in fact yield analyzable information.

The findings will be reported in summary form in respect to the question:

How does the decision-making process which has evolved in the Model Cities Program relate to ethnic minority demands for increased influence in decision-making?

Optimal Conditions for Resident Control

The empirical analysis of the data suggest that residents were able to have significant decision-making roles in: the hiring and firing of Model Cities staff; the allocation of Model Cities budget resources; the initiation of Model Cities projects; and the operation of Model Cities programs when the intensity of resident participation was high. Specifically, the intensity of resident participation was optimal:

1. WHEN RESIDENTS PARTICIPATED IN THE APPLICATION PERIOD FOR A MODEL CITIES GRANT

Of the eleven cities in the sample only one city -- Richmond, California -- had more than a perfunctory role during the application. All the other cities had either a mild role or no real involvement during the application period. Those residents who had a mild role in the application period were able to have some input only after the application was already developed and presented to them for sanctioning. As a whole these residents had a strong negative reaction to a plan which was developed without their consideration, and as a result the city usually made some concession by permitting them to add or amend the application in areas where their concern was most intense. When this situation occurred it seemed to set the stage for confrontation; i.e., an adversary relationship between the residents and the Model Cities administrations. Residents became suspicious of the intents of the Model Cities program and became more active in scrutinizing subsequent planning products and programmatic decisions. On the other hand, in Richmond, where residents were brought in early in the planning stages to develop a Model Cities grant, the resident CDA relationship was generally harmonious. This event was due in large part to the interaction of the professional planners with the residents around those concerns which they wanted addressed by the Model Cities resources. The planners were able to discuss the viable options and the constraints as regarded residents' concerns, as well as revealing the Cities' priorities for the Model Cities resources. An application was developed from this initial interaction and establishment of priorities and concerns from both the residents and the city. As a result, trust between the residents and the city was established, or at least did not become a contentious issue. In fact, this initial interaction, allowed the residents to establish a cooperative relationship with the professional staff of the program and convince the city that the residents should have a role in the selection of the CDA director.

The role of residents in developing the application, then, should be seen as a critical factor for setting the stage for the appropriate pre-conditions for effective resident participation.

2.

In only three of the eleven cities -- Cambridge, Massachusetts; Dayton, Ohio and Richmond, California -- did residents have a significant influence in the selection of the CDA director. With the exception of Richmond, resident influence in the area was due to the insistent pressure of the residents, rather than an input the cities thought was appropriate. In each of these cases residents were prone to support a CDA candidate who seemed to be most sympathetic to their concerns for having a significant role in the program's development and operation. Generally, though, city administrators consistently gave higher priority to a candidate who showed promise of being an efficient administrator of a municipal program. Specifically, a Model Cities director was ultimately chosen by all cities largely on a single criterion -- his ability to "get along" with the city's chief executive. Secondary criteria included his acceptability to the various public and private planning agencies and City Hall in general. It would seem that the last criterion for the ultimate appointment of a CDA director was his ability to get along with the residents.

Given these criteria for ultimate selection by the city's chief executive, most cities considered only those candidates with strong professional and academic backgrounds. Additionally, most of the selected directors were professionals closely related to the original application period. Of the eleven CDA directors, eight were members of the application team for their city; of the eight, three had actually directed the preparation of the application, four others were staff members in the application period, and one worked on the application as a resident.

The overall qualities on which a CDA director was selected bore a minimal relationship to the qualities of leadership which ethnic minority communities seem to require. The criteria on which he was selected and the responsibilities which the municipal chief delegated to him often sabotaged the development of working relationships with the more political segments of the ethnic minority community. In most communities where there was a large ethnic minority population in the MNA, the CDA director was challenged by community organizations to be an advocate for the community's needs. More often than not, these community organizations were frustrated by the inability of the CDA to adequately respond to the community needs as they had perceived them.

In Pittsburgh, the United Black Front, whose members were young and

outside the traditional leadership structure, presented a constant challenge to
the Model Cities Program. From the very first planning year of the Model Cities
Program, the leader of this organization attempted to promote the development of
a neighborhood corporation as an alternative to the Model Cities Program for its
lack of credibility in the community and questioned the commitment of Model
Cities to the black people in the Model Neighborhood area. In this case, the
United Black Front became a constant source of acute frustration to the Model
Cities Program.

In Atlanta, where the mayor directly appointed a CDA head who was
able to adhere to the well-ordered planning schedule of the Model Cities process,
only a small segment of the ethnic minority community was involved in Model
Cities. As a whole many residents did not even know of the program's existence.
Yet at the end of the first action year (two years of actual operation) the CDA
director claimed that the Atlanta Model Cities Program was the "eyes and ears"
of the Model City neighborhoods. When contrasted to the inability of the
Atlanta program to either generate impact on the MNA or the support of its
population, this statement heightened the alienation of many local community
organizations. The CDA director's sense of local sentiment was far inferior to
that of neighborhood organizations whose activities he ignored at best and
branded subversive at worst. Generally, the Model Cities in Atlanta was not
regarded as a bastion of community advocacy. The frustration and increasing
alienation of the residents with the Model Cities Program is captured in an
event which occurred during November of 1970. Residents were demanding responses from the CDA director on certain issues with which they were most concerned.
The CDA director at the time was away on business, and the residents had a
"sleep-in" at the CDA offices. In large part, the residents were concerned with
three basic issues:

1. The CDA was located in the community and yet seemed insensitive
and generally unwilling to assume an advocate posture.

2. The program was not eager to involve residents in decision-making
nor to inform them of its activities.

3. The CDA staff, while largely black, was not of the same class as
the majority of the residents.

As a whole, the residents felt that the lack of their participation in
the program's development and operation was its main flaw. The leader of the
"sleep-in" maintained:

"If no more than a few middle class residents had been involved in planning, if they had not gone into the neighborhood and picked out people they wanted, then it might have worked. You have to meet the needs of poor people first. If Model Cities had done this [involved residents in planning] from the first, then it would have worked because there would have been good ideas. But it started off wrong, so it could not work."[4]

In Gary, the CDA director was also appointed directly by the Mayor. The recently elected mayor was himself anxious that the program not create any additional waves in a political situation which promised to be turbulent. Accordingly the CDA director was charged with steering the Model Cities Program free from potentially political issues. This meant to a large extent playing down resident participation in the program. The CDA director's administrative style limited resident involvement and relied heavily on the intensive efforts of a few professional city staff members. Resident responsibilities were limited largely to the review of program materials. It appeared that most residents acknowledged that Model Cities was a "mayor's program" and relied on their faith in the mayor's sensitivity to ethnic minority residents and their condition in the city.

In Denver, the CDA director was a close friend and political associate of the Mayor. His additional role as special assistant to the mayor maintained the administration of the Model Cities Program high in the echelons of city hall. The close relationship between these two men strongly influenced the Model Cities process as a reflection of the mayor's priorities. Two administrative structures facilitated this occurrence. First, the CDA director sat on the Mayor's cabinet which met weekly to review City operations and provide a forum for the Mayor's executive policies. Second, the CDA director chaired the Urban Resources Development Agency, a super department which oversees the operation of several federally assisted programs including Model Cities. From the first day of his appointment as CDA director his relationship with the residents was strained. They were suspicious of a director whom they had no voice in appointing and who was so closely related to the mayor.

In San Antonio the conflicting allegiance of the CDA director to the chief municipal executive and the residents was a model case. Here again, the director was appointed directly by the municipal chief. The selection of the director reflected on the one hand the pressures in the community for Mexican-American representation in the decision-making process and, on the other hand, the desire of the City Council to have someone loyal to the "Good Government League"[5] responsible for Model Cities. In the eyes of the municipal chief, the CDA director who was chosen satisfied these criteria. He was Mexican-American and a well-known supporter of the "Good Government League". Needless to say, the Mexican-American community resented his appointment. They were convinced that he saw his role as a representative of the city first and as a representative of the Mexican-American community second, if at all. Throughout the time period studied, the feelings grew among many community organizations that the CDA director was not really in touch with the poor people of the community, nor did he represent them.

As the planning and action year progressed, more and more criticism was heard of the CDA director and his ties to the "Good Goverment League". In several critical situations where he had to interact with residents on pressing issues he succeeded only in widening the gap of communication between himself and the residents.

These examples generally highlight what seems to be a "built-in" contradiction of the Model Cities program. On the one hand, the CDA depends on the power and support of the civic majority while at the same time it is expected to perform the role of a champion of the interests of the poor. These interests are increasingly interpreted by the residents themselves to mean a transfer of power to the neighborhood. However, in those cases where residents had a direct and significant input in the selection of the director, conflict between the residents and the CDA was less of a constraint in the operation of the program.

It is important to take into account the phenomenon of distrust with which most ethnic minority members view intervention programs which are allegedly designed to help them. Whenever residents are not given an opportunity to have real input in the selection of the leader of such a program, their suspicions are bound to increase.

3. WHEN RESIDENT PARTICIPATION STRUCTURE WAS REPRESENTATIVE OF THE NEIGHBORHOOD CONSTITUENCY

An examination of the eleven chronologies reveals that only two of the cities (Cambridge and Dayton) were deemed representative of the MNA population. Both of these cities had a cohesive community organizational base prior to the inception of Model Cities. In Cambridge, there were several organizations involved in physical and social planning for what became the MNA. In most of these residents participated actively and a few of the programs were run by the residents themselves. When the plans for a Model Cities program were revealed to the residents, most of the community organizations refused to endorse the Model Cities Program unless they were given complete control. Essentially, this predominantly lower-middle class white community feared that Model Cities was urban renewal in another form, and they were determined to keep their community intact. An ad hoc committee representing the residents (with representative members of the community organizations) was formed to draft a resolution to be presented to the city council stating the terms on which they would agree to the approval of the submission of a Model Cities application. To make sure that the wording of the resolution was both clear and legal, the Cambridge Legal Assistance Office volunteered to assist in the drafting of the resolution. The residents in the MNA were encouraged to call their councilmen to support the resolution. Eventually the resolution was passed by the city council without much discussion. In addition, the entire MNA was asked to ratify the resolution. These events prepared the road for active community participation in the program, and reflected an earnest effort to have a representative resident participation group. All of the representatives on the resident structure were selected by an election in the MNA. Any Model City resident could get his name on the ballot by having a petition signed by twenty-five MN residents. In total, 2,407 votes were cast representing an estimated 40% of the eligible voters -- a very impressive turn-out for a community election.

The important factors which seemed to be related to representativeness of the resident structure was the existence of community organizations which provided participatory experience for residents prior to Model Cities and a pressing issue around which residents and organizations could coalesce. These factors also played a significant role in the resultant representativeness of the resident structure in Dayton. While in Cambridge the pressing issue around which community organizations and residence coalesced was a fear of "urban renewal" destroying their neighborhood, in Dayton the sequence of two major riots, before and during Model Cities, provided the cementing factor for residents. The threat of disturbances and violence was a significant factor influencing the nature of and resolution of the context between MNA residents and the city commission relative to Model Cities resident structure control over Model City policy and decision-making. In an interview of September, 1968, the municipal chief indicated that the riots of 1966 and 1967 had "plenty" of impact on Dayton's officials -- he stated that the foundations of social order were severely shaken in Dayton. Moreover, city officials and some West Dayton spokesmen could see that social control was in tenuous condition following the riots.

These incidents of violence or at least strenuous protest by residents and community organizations at key decision points (particularly during the application period), and the questioning of institutional authority during Model Cities all paved the road for increased decision influence in Model Cities for Dayton's residents.

Representativeness in Dayton was (as in the case in Cambridge) characterized by a strong resident group pressing the city's authorities early in the Model Cities experience for a definitive role of authority. As a result of this demand, most of the MNA residents did not only become more knowledgeable of what Model Cities was about, but were aware of the need to support those residents who were "confronting" city hall. The impetus of the initial campaign by community organizations, supported by the constituencies of previously established community organizations, enabled the establishment of a resident participation group which was not only representative but elevated to the status of "equal partnership" with the city commission. This resolution was a binding contract with the city under which "...the decisions of the Model Cities Planning Council (resident group) hall at all times be given full consideration in all decisions made by the commission affecting the welfare of the area residents."[6]

In both of these cases, then, the representativeness of the resident structure was a result of "a priori" activities on the part of active community organizations to secure a position of strength for their communities in relation to the Model Cities program. Through the combined and coordinated efforts of previously established organizations, wedded by a pervasive issue, the MNA residents were able to gain "poker chips" with which to negotiate. It would seem that a representative structure inherently meant strong community support, that is, a majority of citizens in the affected area supported the positions being taken in relation to City Hall.

Most of the cities in the study sample, however, had a "minimally" to "not representative" resident structure. In these cities there seems to be a general pattern associated with this occurrence:

1. There were no strong community organizations previous to Model Cities which afforded the residents participatory experience with intervention programs. As a result, those community residents who sanctioned the Model Cities program did not represent a contentious force to city.

2. There were strong community organizations previous to Model Cities, but these groups were at odds with each other, and as a result dissipated their collective strength in relation to city hall and to community support for their efforts.

4. WHEN THE RESIDENTS HAD ACTUAL SUBSTANTIVE ROLES IN ESTABLISHING THE ADMINISTRATIVE ORGANIZATION AND PREROGATIVES OF THE CDA STRUCTURE AND THE RESIDENT STRUCTURE

Most of the cities had either an "active" or a "mild" role with regard to this variable, though only two had a "dominant" role. As might be discerned, these are the areas where the actual ground rules circumscribing the relationship between residents and the city are laid out. Additionally, in the sequence of events in the Model Cities process, these episodes occur early and in fact set the pattern of the relationship between residents and city hall which emerges. Those residents who were able to establish a "dominant role" with regard to these variables did so early in the Model Cities process. In both cases the residents pushed for and received a city resolution outlining the areas of responsibilities of the resident participation structure which was binding throughout the period studied.

Those cities which had an "active role" in establishing the ground rules outlining their prerogatives fell short of their desired goals and often settled for compromised relationships. The resistance of the municipality to a role of increased decision-making for the resident structure was often stronger than the initiatives of the residents.

In San Antonio, for instance, two of the more active community organizations strongly protested that the resident participation structure established was merely an advisory committee. The resident organization was assigned the role of reviewing Model Cities overall plans and operations. Delegated to the resident group were nine professional planners and technicians who were to assist the resident organization in reviewing the plans and to help develop plans for component areas. In total, this group consisted of eighteen (18) residents and nine (9) professionals. No rules were ever established on the relations of the citizens and the technicians. If the residents had any disagreements with a recommendation of the professional technical group, they simply ignored it -- eventually to find out that the recommendation was acted upon by the CDA director. There were, in general, no procedures for referring matters back to the professional technical group. This lack of definition in roles produced tension between the levels of the Model Cities organization. Similar tension existed between the resident group and the city council, which had never defined the resident organization's authority or its role. There was no procedure for mutual consultation between the resident organizations and city hall -- nor between the residents and the professional technicians.

The activity on the part of residents to define their roles and prerogatives more clearly was met with resistance. The CDA director made no attempts during the first few months of the program to respond to these issues. When he did respond he stated that the Model Cities contract was between the Department of Housing and Urban Development and the city and thus the city had final authority. He implied that the residents had none. This notion was constantly promoted in the city council by the chief executive (who from the beginning was not anxious to have a Model Cities program in San Antonio). He reminded the city council that it possessed the final authority and responsibility for the Model Cities program and did not need to look to any group before it made a final decision. Although, unfortunately, he was legally correct, this opinion ignores the fact that HUD also requires a functioning resident participation structure below the city council to formulate policies and pass on recommendations. San Antonio did not have such a structure. There existed a tremendous distrust between the resident group and the professional technicians. Many residents felt that their plans were not presented by the professional technicians to the city council in the form in which they had been approved.

In the period studied residents were not able to have their roles established any more clearly or substantively. The activity on the part of the residents, however, did make the CDA and the city council aware that there was a significant resident concern around this issue. Eventually the city council promised to abide by the resident organization's wishes while retaining for itself the power to override those wishes should it see fit. The city council made it clear that they had the power to turn down a project which had already been approved by the resident group; it was not clear however whether the city council also assumed they could pass a project on if it had been rejected by the resident organization.

5.   WHEN RESIDENTS RECEIVED CONTINUAL AND DIRECT INFORMATION ON MODEL CITIES MATTERS FROM THE CDA OFFICE.

Of the eleven cities, three (Cambridge, Dayton and Richmond) had instituted a relatively good procedure for transmitting information to the resident structure. In all three cases, residents were able to secure good working relationships with the professional planning staff of the program. In Richmond, for example, the process of involving professional planners (usually part-time line agency representatives) at times resulted in what might be called "reverse co-optation". While some of the professional staff became defensive and angry during the initial confrontation periods and left, never to return, others became committed to helping the residents in their planning efforts and in effect became advocate planners. Largely due to the commitment of the CDA director and his staff to meaningful resident participation, the professionals took great time and pains to explain and brief the citizen structure on those matters they were to vote on or endorse. In San Antonio, on the other hand, there was tremendous resistance on the part of professional planners to "plan with residents". It seemed to them that endless time was taken up "explaining the fundamentals". As a result many of the planning products, applications, and other planning components were presented to the residents hurriedly and without appropriate notice. The submission of a General Neighborhood Renewal Plan to obtain additional funds from HUD was given to the resident structure one day before the alleged deadline. Yet, the resident structure was urged to vote and sanction this application or face the possibility of losing needed additional funding. In effect, this lack of continual communication and transmission of information to the resident group meant that residents could be safely ignored.

A similar pattern emerged in Pittsburgh where professional planners dominated the discussions between themselves and residents by informing the residents as to their plans and proposals for the MNA without permitting feedback from residents.

In Atlanta, although the planning coordinator was committed to a form of advocacy planning, he found out that there was strong resistance to this style of planning from those planners on loan from other agencies. In addition, there was little or no procedure to "plug-in" residents with planners. Each planner, responsible to a component area, had his own idea as to how to go about interacting with residents to obtain their ideas and involve them with planning. In general, though, all felt ill at ease with residents, and thought that resident participation usurped too much time that could be used to do "real planning".

6.   WHEN THE MODEL CITIES PROGRAM WAS LOCATED IN A SMALL CITY (LESS THAN 325,000) WHICH HAD A SMALL ETHNIC MINORITY POPULATION (BELOW 15% OF THE TOTAL CITY POPULATION) AND WAS GOVERNED BY A CITY MANAGER TYPE OF MUNICIPAL ADMINISTRATION

This condition represents the collective impact of the intervening variables labeled "ENVIRONMENT I" on the intensity of resident participation. The data suggests that ethnic minorities in large cities governed by a strong-mayor type of municipal government tended to gain less influence in the decision-making processes. Of the eleven cities, five fall into this category: Atlanta, Detroit, Denver, Pittsburgh and Gary, (San Antonio might also be considered in this category).[7] As a whole this finding provides definite indication that ethnic minority residents were unable to use the participatory mechanisms to increase their influence in decision-making.

In all of these cities the municipal chief had the most influence in the selection of not only the CDA director, but also the agencies and professionals who would direct the course of the program. Usually this meant that the entire Model Cities application was written within city hall. The scope of resident participation, the focus for the Model Cities resources, the boundary of the MNA, and the line agencies to be involved in the development and execution of programs, were largely predetermined before there was actual resident input. In general, the final application reflected the traditional planning methodologies and biases of city agencies who were not accustomed to nor had any desire to plan with residents.

Large city mayors were particularly sensitive to their dominant political constituencies when and if resident dissatisfaction with Model Cities created some political turbulence. In Detroit, for example, the mayor was an enthusiastic supporter of Model Cities, even before the program was actually passed by Congress. Yet the task force assembled by the mayor to develop an application was noticeably lacking of resident input. After the application was written and submitted, the director of the Community Renewal Program (a city urban renewal agency which was charged with the responsibility with heading the task force) held several meetings in the community to familiarize residents with the document. Upon realizing that they were locked into a program into which they had no input and which was headed by the "urban renewal agency" to which they were hostile, the residents organized a protest to oppose the Model Cities program. Later they drew up an alternative citizen participation plan which not only proposed a stronger resident role in Model Cities, but also required that all urban renewal activities in the designated MNA be halted until they could be reviewed by the resident participation group. This activity on the part of the residents to promote this alternative plan came as a surprise to the mayor. As a result, the mayor was less enthusiastic about the program. He made very few public appearances for the program and failed to use his authority over other city agencies in its behalf. Although the residents were able to get their alternative citizen participation plan partially implemented (they were not given the prerogative to review urban renewal activity in the MNA), they were unable to establish a strong decision-making role in the Model Cities program. At the end of the period studied residents felt their role had been pre-empted; they grew increasingly frustrated with the program and simply became apathetic.

In general, then, large city mayors seemed too unwilling and uncommitted to the goals of resident participation to suffer the inevitable challenges of ethnic minorities for change in the city government. The result is that resident participation for ethnic minorities has been a frustrating experience in these cities. Resident participation as a vehicle for control does not seem feasible in large urban cities. The initiatives undertaken by the "powerless" to redefine "widespread citizen participation" in terms of a redistribution of decision-making authority were not, as a whole, successful. On the other hand, it would seem that the actions of large city mayors to operationally define "resident participation" in a non-threatening manner to their own political hegemony prevailed.

7.   WHEN THE MODEL CITIES PROGRAM WAS LOCATED IN A CITY WHICH HAD
        EXPERIENCED RACIAL DISTURBANCES PRIOR AND/OR DURING THE MODEL CITIES
        PROGRAM AND WHICH HAD A COHESIVE COMMUNITY ORGANIZATION BASE

This condition represents the collective impact of the intervening variables labeled "ENVIRONMENT II". Previously it was noted that this condition was characteristic of the case in Dayton, Ohio. The increasing organization of the ghetto residents and the momentum of the ghetto riots influenced the city commission and the city manager to more readily acquiesce to the demands of ghetto leaders. Coming when they did, the riots significantly influenced the city's planning and decision-making processes. They were prompted to respond to a confrontation style of negotiation with those community organizations and leaders representing the MNA. Choices between incremental change through existing institutions and more rapid change invariably were decided in favor of the latter. In effect, this environment facilitated the use of the participatory mechanisms which emerged as a vehicle for strong resident influence in Model Cities decision-making processes.

In general the occurrence of racial disturbances during the Model Cities program stimulated MNA residents and community organizations to take a more aggressive confrontation posture in regards to the Model Cities program.

Residents usually reacted to racial disturbances during Model Cities in two important ways. First, there was an apparent increase in their willingness to listen to the more "militant" groups in the community. Second, there was a tendency to turn away from existing programs being utilized in the Model Neighborhood area. These two reactions encouraged MNA residents to place a great emphasis on local community control of existing community programs (including MC) and to press for economic development of their communities.

It seems then that the promotion of a definition of "widespread citizen participation" in terms of increased decision-making roles for the "have-nots" was partly facilitated by social disturbances.

1. The significant level of the Pearsonian product - moment correlation coefficient (r) for an N of 11 and (N-2) 9 degrees of freedom is .602. This is the significant level for a two-tailed test, which was used in this study since the direction of all the variable correlations was not assumed.

2. Baggaley, Andrew, Intermediate Correlational Methods, John Wiley and Sons, Inc., New York, New York, 1964. pp. 60-66.

3. Although the significant level is .602, the coefficient of /.59/ is assumed to be sufficiently approximate to .602 to be also considered significant.

4. Atlanta Chronologies, Vol. III, p. 63.

5. The Good Government League is a strong political organization in San Antonio dedicated to the goals of eliminating corruption and providing sound municipal government. For the last twenty years the majority of the city councilmen have been members of this organization.

6. Dayton Chronologies, Vol. II, p. 9.

7. San Antonio generally falls into this category also although it is governed by a city manager type of government. It is the largest city in the United States governed by a city manager executive. The city council is composed of nine members, elected at large, and is chaired by the mayor, who is selected as the mayor. The "real politic" of the government, though, is largely determined by the conservative influence of the "Good Government League". The head of the league had been Mayor McCallister, who coincidentally was selected mayor for several terms. In addition, for the last seventeen years the majority of the councilmen have been members of the Good Government League.

CHAPTER VI

CONCLUSIONS

In previous chapters the history and context which influenced the
institutionalization of "widespread citizen participation" was recounted.
Fully aware of the controversies which centered around citizen participation
as it was operationalized in previous federal intervention programs, Model
Cities program developers did not formulate their program along similar participation formats. Rather than developing a new institution outside of the
system such as the Community Action Agencies, an administrative structure
directly responsible to the municipal chief was charged with the primary responsibility of the program's operation. Indeed, this new institution - the
City Demonstration Agency - was created to circumvent the previous experience
of the CAP agencies. Rather than having an indirect role, and minimal control
in the programs operation, the municipal chiefs were to have a significant
leadership role over the Model Cities program. The underlying reasons for
this strategy was to increase the effectiveness of the program in what Roland
Warren refers to as the 4 Cs.[1]

> ... <u>Comprehensiveness</u> - projects of the Model Cities program were
> to be developed in a wide range of different sectors such as
> health care, education, housing, manpower training, transporta-
> tion, etc.
>
> ... <u>Concentration</u> - resources and projects were to be concentrated
> in a limited and circumscribed Model Neighborhood area so as
> to maximize the outcome of the programs input in a specified
> area.
>
> ... <u>Coordination</u> - The City Demonstration Agency, under the leader-
> ship of the municipal chief, would act as a coordinating umbrella
> under which the various federal and state programs, projects, and
> resources operating in the MNA could be synchronized.
>
> ... <u>Citizen participation</u> - In pursuing the above objectives, there
> was to be "widespread citizen participation".

This study is concerned with the latter area of the Model Cities programs. Although the Department of Housing and Urban Development were unambiguous
in respect to the role the municipal chiefs were to play in the program, the

113

specific form of "widespread citizen participation" was to be defined by the particular social and political dynamics of the locality. There were, of course, a set of performance standards for "widespread citizen participation", but as previously noted they were suggestive rather than prescriptive, permissive rather than restrictive. In large measure, as H. Ralph Taylor stated, the outcome of the Model Cities Program (and thus inherently the form of citizen participation) would be determined by the "... will and competence of the communities to meet the problems of the slums.[2] It is this undefined field -" "... the will and competence of communities to meet the problems of the slums" - which this study attempts to understand. An attempt was made to identify and quantify most of the factors associated with the "will of communities" and to determine their relationship to the kind of "widespread citizen participation" which evolved in the city.

Generally, the kind or level of resident participation which evolved were subject both to the will and competence of the city on the one hand, and that of the residents in the community on the other. But in fact the residents, the "have-nots" of the slums of American Cities are at a distinct disadvantage with regard to institutionalized norms of competence. Their will is to have more control over the programs and municipal decisions which affect their lives. Sherri Arnstein, in an article entitled "Maximum Feasible Manipulation" written in behalf of the residents of the Model Cities Program in Philadelphia, noted that the residents in the Model Cities area are like players invited to a poker game and given less chips than other players.[3] She observed in another article, "Ladder of Citizen Participation" that many of the cities chief executives correctly expressed their will as they "...interpreted the HUD provisions for access to the decision-making process as the escape hatch they sought to relegate citizens to the traditional advisory role."[4]

Using the sociology of knowledge as an analytical framework, Chapter Two underscored the tendency of the "have-nots" to refuse relegation to mere advisory roles. Where municipal governments and official policy makers sought to impose a traditional definition and limitation of the participation concept, ethnic minorities have sought, through the recognition of their collective identity, to define participation in terms of self-determination. There is, in essence, a conflict between the systematic notion of participation and that of the "have-nots". Robert A. Aleshire points out that, it is ironic to consider the federal government making allowances in a federal program which would "give" power to residents in a participatory sense: "The history of the last decade has been that citizen participation within the context of guidelines and values imposed by federal administrators and the Congress is the reflection of the mores of the country. Participation has meant in the fashion, form and mix which would not basically question these overall tenants."[5] The theoretical analysis of Chapter Two sought to highlight the dynamic implication of this observation with regard to the aims of ethnic minorities to increase their participatory influence.

Against this background, perhaps the most obvious outcome of the Model Cities Program is its failure to promote, encourage, stimulate or lead urban institutions to meet the needs of ethnic minority groups. In part, this failure can be seen as an overestimation on the part of HUD of the "will and competence of communities to meet the problems of slums". This was seen, as one of the basic reasons why earlier phases of the reform movement (Gray Area Program, PCVD, CAP, et. al.) failed to accomplish their overall objective. Or, in general, it could be the result of inaccurate assumptions and analysis which underlie participation policies (or the program as a whole). Or, even more seriously, this failure may be the result of an underestimation of the factors and conditions which make up the will of ethnic minorities to "control their own destiny."

It seems that the thinking, assumptions and reasoning behind the Model Cities Program has not only pushed the program in the direction of the already established "powerholders", but also structurally failed to provide the directorship of the program with the strength of viable community leadership. The CDA director's dilemma of conflicting allegiance to city hall and neighborhood groups lessened the programs potential to effectively address itself to the deprivations of ethnic minorities as a whole. Even where a CDA director and his staff was sympathetic to the concerns of the residents for a significant decision-making role, the anxiety to meet programming and funding deadlines, to carry out the planning, budgeting and administrative functions, made it virtually impossible for them to commit themselves to the necessary task of actively organizing the community to insure effective participation. Moreover, insofar as the municipal chief has the final say on the selection of the CDA director, it is unlikely that the selected director would have the strong Black sentiment which might be necessary to earn the support of the "community". This is especially true in large urban communities.

These observations, in addition to the findings of other students of the participation issue earlier cited, seriously put into question the organizational potential of the CDA structure and its management to act as the primary impact agent of the problems of deprivation in ethnic minority communities. It might be argued that the CDA may not be the primary impact agent, neither now nor in the future, and that the planning activities of the CDA are really secondary to other "power interest" in the city. The effectiveness of the planned programs themselves are most likely to be predetermined by outside forces over which the CDA has relatively little control. In general the people who carry out the responsibility for the program (including the CDA director) are followers, not leaders, in the design of the basic change that Model Cities should stand for: decision-making by residents _with_ rather than _by_ bureaucrats and professionals.

To some extent, the failure of the Model Cities Program to reach the majority of the lower class ethnic minority population might be correlated to this problem of leadership. Like most previous federal intervention efforts, Model Cities have mainly attracted a small segment of the ethnic minority community, the great majority of which are already geared toward a middle-class-value orientation. As a result, the program has tended to attract a cadre of "upwardly mobile" types who have alienated the majority of the lower-class ethnic population rather than actively increased its cohesion.

Traditional Planning and Resident Participation

One of the most obvious factors contributing to the continuing state of poverty among ethnic minorities is their virtual exclusion from effective political life in the United States as a whole and in their own communities in particular. Therefore, any real effort to deal with the problem of poverty should recognize and assess the factors and forces which have prevented the effective participation of ethnic minorities in the decisions that directly affect their lives. The requirement of "widespread citizen participation" as an integral part of the Model Cities process has not been given the necessary emphasis on which its operational success depends. From the early stages of the program's development, the goal of resident participation was not given high priority. On the contrary, it was played down by the Model Cities planners. They saw resident participation as somewhat incompatible with the full use of the "rational" planning process they had developed. To this extent a viable process for insuring the effective participation of area residents was a victim of the "traditional planning" approach or what Herbert Gans calls the "method oriented" planning approach.[6] This approach holds tightly to the security of accepted planning methods and techniques and in so doing often loses sight of the goals which the methods are intended to achieve. Gans might argue that if "widespread citizen participation" was a primary goal of Model Cities, the traditional planning approaches are incompatible with its achievement. A more appropriate method might be what Gans calls the "problem-oriented methods",[7] which concentrate on the people and on the social, political, and economic forces which foster their deprivation, rather than on the neighborhood conditions which are themselves consequences of these forces.

Model Cities planning schemes, however, have largely concentrated their efforts on instituting mechanisms and processes to affect the economies of coordination of state and federal resources. Cities largely depended on the inputs of their own professional planners, who themselves have traditionally resisted planning with the residents. This occurrence can be related to the assumption that the key to a successful attack on the problems of urban blight and poverty is to structure the resources and control of the program in the hands of City Hall. If the assumptions of the "reform movement" were correct; i.e., that the institutions traditionally charged with the amelioration of poverty are ineffectual, this strategy does not reflect an understanding of the political forces which foster the deprivation of ethnic minorities. The reaction of Mayor Addonizio, as described earlier, is generally the response given to ethnic minorities "demand" for increased participation in the urban political system. More important, the consequences of this strategy raises the questions of how a national intervention program designed to attack the blight of urban cities as a whole, to benefit the society in general and to ameliorate the sense of powerlessness of the poor and ethnic minorities, is prevented from becoming responsive only to the values of those who actually run the programs; i.e., the bureaucrats and professional planners.

One immediate answer might be to enact stronger resident participation performance standards. For if "widespread citizen participation is to be a viable goal, it would seem that performance standards with more "muscle" would be appropriate. Prescriptive language which requires particular roles for residents in each phase of the program's operation would be more effective than performance standards which are left to interpretation by local urban governments. In addition, performance standards with more "muscle" are likely to increase the leverage of the "powerless" seeking a role in the decision making. Just as important it would seem that performance standards which allow local governments who are not interested in encouraging resident participation would place less emphasis on the attainment of effective participation as a goal.

Impact of "Widespread Citizen Participation" on the Ethnic Minority Communities

What impact was there upon the attitudes of residents towards government and towards the Model Cities Program? Direct answers to these questions, though not the primary focus of this study, might be projected from the general findings as well as from the studies of other students of the participation issue.

As a whole, residents were extremely distrustful of the sincerity of a program run by city hall which allegedly had as a goal ameliorating the factors which binded them in poverty. Their distrust became even more acute as the CDA director and the professional planners manifested an inability to respond to their needs, or to fully integrate their inputs into the final planning products. Moreover, it seems that significant resident input to the planning process occurred largely as a result of political pressure exerted through the protest actions of the residents. Realistically, but unfortunately, this tendency suggests that some degree of violence is inevitable to the acquisition of increased decision-making roles for the "have-nots". It seems that this tendency strongly convinced many members of the ethnic minority community that racism is so entrenched and pervasive in this country that more often than not, the greatest power they have is the power to disrupt. Ralph Kramer, among others, suggests that federal policies affecting the welfare of deprived citizens have been more significantly affected by riots than by the positive operation of resident participation in intervention programs.[8]

Insofar as it has increased distrust or failed to coordinate the interest of the "have-nots" with the general interest of city hall, Model Cities has had a negative impact. To the extent that residents might have been forced to assume a confrontation posture with city hall as a primary strategy for extracting benefits from the program, the program has increased distrust and vitiated its ability to relate to the needs of the community. Residents of the Philadelphia Model Cities Program concluded at the end of their unsuccessful effort to increase their decision-making influence in that program:

"You can't trust city hall or HUD. That's what the Nixon

Administration ignores when it pronounces from on high that the goal of citizen participation is to 'build trust' between city hall and the community.

"It might be beautiful if city hall and HUD were trustworthy. But our history testifies to the fact that we'd be fools to trust the politicians. We were cheated each time we let our legal guard down. We only succeeded when we insisted that the politicians live up to their promises, and when we demonstrated that we had some power.

"All four Model City directors used us to achieve their own ends. Each was willing to negotiate with us when he assumed the job and had some important HUD deadline to meet. Right after that goal had been achieved, each tried to renege on the partnership agreement by creating an outrageous crisis around the renewal of our contract. Though some of the staff of the city and federal agencies were clearly honest and helpful, most of them lied, equivocated, cheated and distorted.

"HUD itself has demonstrated that it can't be trusted. Its official guidelines admitted that existing institutions have historically failed the community. It said that the cities had to demonstrate willingness to innovate if they wanted the Model Cities money. It promised that Washington would not dictate the methods to be used because it wanted cities to create their own strategies for social change. Though HUD never advocated community control as a strategy for institutional change, it officially endorsed power sharing with the citizens as an experimental strategy.

"So what happened? We took those guidelines at face value and struggled to achieve power sharing with our city. We were one of the few communities in the country with a sufficient community power base to get the city to agree to our demands. HUD put its seal of approval on our agreement. Despite many attempts by the City to subvert it, we managed to hang in. Through thousands of hours of blood, sweat, and tears, we managed to negotiate a plan which had some genuine promise for community renewal. The plan clearly articulated that the basic strategy for achieving lasting social change is to shift the balance of power between exploiter and exploited. The mayor approved the plan and sent the plan to Washington. Then, HUD, the big White Father, violated that agreement by announcing that the new Administration (with its limited wisdom about intercity communities) thought it was too risky for the mayor and wanted it changed! The mayor happily agreed and submitted a different strategy without even consulting us! And HUD claims not to understand why people like us feel that they use maximum feasible manipulation."[9]

In terms of economic impact, Model Cities cannot claim a great measure of success. Bennet Harrison's research on the extent to which Model Cities increased employment of ethnic minorities concluded that the urban poor did not receive its adequate share of Model Cities resources or jobs.* Briefly summarized here are his study findings:[10]

    ... Citizen Boards were active in most cities. Yet relatively few of their members received actual salaries.

    ... Model Neighborhood residents shared in the direct, salaried employment created by the program. They worked as professionals' aides, in a host of clerical office jobs, as foremen, and as laborers. They were least represented in the first category: less than a quarter of all Model City professionals during the planning period actually lived in the target area. They were best represented among the paraprofessionals; about two-thirds of these workers were MN residents. Their share of the clerical/office jobs seems especially disappointing: only 49 percent. Here there's no excuse (or at least, there are fewer plausible excuses) relating to the allegedly "heavy skill requirements normal to a start-up period."

    ... Even after removing the effects of age, sex, education, hours and occupation, it was still apparent that MN residents received $800 - $1,300 less per year than outsiders. We also learned that whites earn somewhat higher salaries than minorities regardless of residence.

    ... CDAs appear to recruit a disproportionate number of MN women relative to men and to place considerable weight on educational credentials, even for jobs as clerical positions for which actual technical requirements are considered to be relatively modest.

    ... In general, the CDAs located in the Richmond-Boston megalopolis have allocated larger proportions of their jobs to MN residents than has been true for projects in other parts of the country.

    ... The quantitative evidence assessed in this paper suggest that once again the urban poor have not received as large a share as

---

* Harrison's study employs multivariate analysis to investigate the rates of employment of ghetto residents and the salaries of all Model Cities employees during the program's planning period. His sample consisted of "first round" cities, nine of which (Richmond, Denver, Gary, Cambridge, Detroit, Rochester, Dayton, San Antonio, Pittsburgh) were cities in the present study sample.

possible of the benefits associated with a government program ostensibly directed to improving their welfare.

These are among the reasons why many members in the black and other ethnic communities see the Model Cities program as enhancing the conditions which foster a "para-colonial" relationship rather than being an agent to promote autonomy or yield increased benefits to the ghetto community. Ralph A. Metcalf in an article entitled "Chicago Model Cities and Neocolonization" in the April, 1970 issue of the Black Scholar magazine, wrote:

> "...the community itself received little if any benefit from these programs. Moreover, these liberal pacifiers took a devastating psychological toll on the masses of black people in this country by increasing their physical dependence on a system which has exploited and oppressed them for over 440 years. This pacification is a form of neocolonialism."

Sam Yette's national best seller, The Choice, is another account which supports the notion that national intervention efforts have had a "colonizing" impact on ethnic minority communities.

> "The Great Society pacification programs, then, must be judged as failures, both in the honesty of their designs and in their truer aims of placating people justly aroused. In view of their maximum goals, the fund and the personnel provided, and the authority to do the job, the OEO and civil rights program did not relinquish the original aims of white establishment exploitation. They left ultimate control and financial benefits with the colonialists - not with the colonized; nor even were control and profits shared equitably between them."[11]

Of course "widespread citizen participation" has also had some positive impact on ethnic minorities' communities, as recounted in Chapter Three. The most positive impact has been the exposure of communities to the complexities and subtleties of governmental activities and operations. The active participation of the residents in the political arena in urban localities has provided a learning experience, a legitimate (though limiting) forum through which they have been able to express their needs, and coalesce their efforts for a change. One thing is certain, though, ethnic minorities are realizing that the present institutional order will not change itself, and therefore, they have accepted the onus of change. In many ghetto communities, ethnic minorities are bringing about a change of minds through the "process of black-resocialization," a change which they hope will in turn bring about a change in their situation in the social system.

Future of Resident Participation in National Intervention Efforts

The history of resident participation in national intervention efforts have followed the trend of a normal distribution curve. From the early 50s, when citizen participation was essentially defined by blue ribbon committees of volunteers or appointees, to the President's Committee on Juvenile Delinquency, to the OEO War on Poverty, and finally to the Model Cities Program, citizen participation has experienced its rise and its decline. While the poor and ethnic minorities have increased their political sophistication over this period, the legislative enactments to encourage resident participation seem to become increasingly constraining. As previously noted, "widespread citizen participation" represents a retreat from resident participation as encouraged in the Community Action Programs. The emphasis on planning and coordination, the limitations on the organizational body which could assume the functions of the CDA, and the "return" of authority to local government combined to decrease the emphasis on and concern with resident participation in the Model Cities Program. More recently, the Nixon Administration has instituted measures to limit the prerogatives of target area communities to traditional advisory and revisionary roles. John Strange noted that in May, 1969 a CDA letter forbade resident groups to exclusively initiate projects and required all Model City Agencies to assure HUD that in no case would "the city's ability to take responsibility for developing the plan" be impeded.[12] The revenue sharing programs of the administration, aimed at easing city budgets, included absolutely none of the 1960 language about "community participation." Under the current administration, then, the prospects of the federal government encouraging resident participation are dim. Despite the seemingly increasing limitations of the degree and extent of resident participation as provided in citizen participation requirements, the call of ethnic minorities for "community control" is set on a course which will not be re-routed. As Melvin Moguloff points out:

> "In some Model Cities, no matter what the new Federal Policy, the character of the accommodation between black neighborhood leadership and city government will not permit a return to milder forms of citizen participation."[13]

Some students of the participation issue suggest that neither the Democratic Administration of President Kennedy nor that of President Johnson intended the "have-nots" of the urban slums to gain as much decision-making influence as they did or at least so much influence as to present a real or imagined threat to local government. Moynihan asserts, in fact, that it was a mistake that led the federal government to stimulate resident activity in this direction.[14] Others suggest that the Democratic party sought to placate and integrate the urban poor with the "Great Society Programs" during the turbulent years of the 1960s.[15] In either case the prognosis for "resident participation", at least from the federal viewpoint, seems to be an abandonment or a strong de-emphasis of the requirement. But the problem of economic and political deprivation of the poor and ethnic minorities remains, and is perhaps the most critical issue in this society.

The main dilemma, it would seem, involving the controversies of resident participation is the incompatibility (alleged) between "resident participation" and "coordination". The solution offered by Marris & Rein and more recently promoted by Howard W. Hallman is perhaps more viable than the present organizational arrangements for resident participation. They suggest the creation of two separate organizations, one to carry out the functions of coordination, and the other resident participation (and other community development projects). Specifically, Hallman suggests that as a needed extension of this democratic system, the federal government should support the activity of the "have-nots" who are seeking to become more fully integrated in governmental processes:

> "From this philosophy flows the notion that federal funds can appropriately go to a local organization that has as its purpose the development of citizen self-help capacity through resident-controlled neighborhood institutions. Since this function can not be easily performed by the municipal instrument for program coordination, as we have seen, a separate organization is needed. Such an organization could be a part of city government, or it might be a quasi-public agency organized as a private, non-profit corporation. It should be governed by a board which represents various elements of the community, including local government, leaders of the 'establishment', and representatives of the persons served. Its chief purpose would not be to deliver services but rather to assist residents to organize and conduct their own activities. Thus, its functions would include technical assistance, training, and monitoring of the funds flowing through it to neighborhood organizations. This outline, of course, describes the Community Action Agency, shorn of the coordination task which it cannot perform anyway and revitalized to focus clearly on the mission of citizen development."[16]

Of course, no government can be expected to organize against itself. In the end, what is expected is that the government of a democratic society recognize how remote its large and most influential institutions are from their clients and support new institutional organizations to deal more responsively with them. Freedom in the unique conditions of the "powerless" in American society means that they must have the choice between participation in the larger society and in their own independent structures.

Footnotes - Chapter VI:

1. The Model Cities Program - Assumptions - Experience - Implications - paper presented at the Annual Forum Program, National Conference on Social Welfare, Dallas, Texas, May 17, 1971, p. 8-10.

2. Model Cities Service Center Bulletin, A Report on Progress (special issue), Vol. 2, No. 9 - 1971; p. 6.

3. Sherri Arnstein, Public Administration Review, Special Issue, Vol. XXXII, September, 1972.

4. Sherri Arnstein, Article in AIP Journal, "Ladder of Citizen Participation", p. 220, July, 1969.

5. Robert A. Aleshire, "Power to the People; An Assessment of the Community Action and Model Cities Experience", Public Administration Review - Vol. XXXII, September, 1972. Special Issue.

6. Herbert Gans, "Social and Physical Planning for the Elimination of Urban Poverty" in: Bernard J. Frieden and Robert Morris (eds), Urban Planning and Social Policy, Basic Books, Inc., Publishers, New York, p. 49.

7. Herbert Gans, op. cit., p. 51.

8. Ralph Kramer, Participation of the Poor; Englewood Cliffs, New Jersey, Prentice-Hall, 1969, p. 273.

9. Sherri Arnstein, "Maximum Feasible Manipulation in Philadelphia - What The Power Structure Did To Us" (as told to Sherri Arnstein); City (magazine of urban life and environment); October/November, 1970 - p.37.

10. Bennet Harrison, "The Participation of Ghetto Residents in the Model Cities Program," AIP Journal, January, 1973.

11. Samuel F. Yette, The Choice: The Issue of Black Survival in America, G. P. Rutman's Sons, New York, 1971; p. 39.

12. John Strange, "The Impact of Citizen Participation on Public Administration", Public Administration Review (Special Issue); Vol. XXXII; September, 1972, p. 464.

13. Melvin B. Mogulof, Citizen Participation: "A Review and Commentary on Federal Policies and Practices" (Washington, D.C., the Urban Institute, 1970), mimeo; Part I, p. 80.

14. Moynihan, op. cit., p. 87.

15. Francis Fox Riven; Richard A. Cloward; Regulating the Poor: The Functions of Public Welfare, Vintage Books, New York, Chapter 9 ("The Great Society and Relief; Federal Intervention").

16. Howard W. Hallman, "Federally Financed Citizen Participation," Public

Administration Review (Special Issue); Vol. XXXII, September, 1972; p. 426.

DATA COLLECTION SCHEDULE

City _____

1-   INTERVENING VARIABLES (ENVIRONMENTAL)

A.   SIZE OF THE CITY

                                                    _____ THOUSAND
                                                    _____
                                                    _____

        COMMENTS

B.   TYPE OF MUNICIPAL GOVERNMENT

                    _____   CITY MANAGER (WEAK MAYOR)
                    _____   CITY MANAGER (ELECTED MAYOR-NON-PARTISAN)
                    _____   MAYOR (ELECTED AT LARGE-PARTISAN)

        COMMENTS

C. RACE AND ETHNIC COMPOSITION OF CITY

                    _____   % OF WHITES
                    _____   % OF BLACKS
                    _____   % OF SPANISH SURNAME

        COMMENTS

D. RACE AND ETHNIC COMPOSITION OF MODEL NEIGHBORHOOD AREA

                    _____   % OF WHITES
                    _____   % OF BLACKS
                    _____   % OF SPANISH SURNAME

        COMMENTS

E.   POPULATION OF MNA

_____   THOUSAND

_____

_____

COMMENTS

11   INTERVENING VARIABLES

A.   ARE THERE ANY REPORTED INCIDENCES OF CIVIL DISORDERS IN THE FIVE YEAR
     PERIOD PRIOR TO THE PLANNING YEAR

_____   YES

_____   NO

COMMENTS

B.   ARE THERE ANY REPORTED INCIDENCES OF CIVIL DISORDERS DURING THE TWO YEAR
     PERIOD UNDER STUDY

_____   YES

_____   NO

COMMENTS

C.   WERE THE DISORDERS OF A RACIAL CHARACTER

_____   YES

_____   NO

COMMENTS

D.   IF THERE WERE MORE THAN ONE IDENTIFY DATE OF EACH OCCURANCE.

COMMENTS

E. WAS ANY ONE KILLED DURING THE DISORDERS

_____ YES

_____ NO

COMMENTS

F. WERE THE VICTIMS, IF ANY, MEMBERS OF AN ETHNIC MINORITY GROUP

_____ YES

_____ NO

2. SOCIAL AND POLITICAL COHESIVENESS OF ETHNIC GROUPS IN THE MNA PRIOR TO THE PLANNING YEAR

A. DOES THE MKGK CASE STUDIES REPORT THE PRESENCE OF ACTIVE ETHNIC COMMUNITY ORGANIZATIONS

_____ YES

_____ NO

COMMENTS

B. IF YES, LIST THESE ORGANIZATIONS

_____

_____

_____

COMMENTS

C. WERE THESE ORGANIZATIONS LINKED TO OTHER FEDERAL OR STATE FUNDED COMMUNITY INTERVENTION EFFORTS? WHICH ONES?

_____

_____

_____

COMMENTS

D. WERE THESE ORGANIZATIONS BASICALLY LOCAL COMMUNITY ORGANIZATIONS NOT SIGNIFICANTLY SPONSORED BY FEDERAL AND/OR STATE FUNDS? WHICH ONES?

129

_____

_____

_____

COMMENTS

E. WITH RESPECT TO EACH ORGANIZATION, DOES THE CASE STUDIES AND OTHER RELATED
MATERIAL INDICATE THAT ANY OF THESE ORGANIZATIONS ENJOYED:

                 _____ STRONG SUPPORT IN THE MNA COMMUNITY

                 _____ MILD SUPPORT IN THE MNA COMMUNITY

                 _____ LOW SUPPORT IN THE MNA COMMUNITY

COMMENTS

F. DOES THE CASE STUDIES AND OTHER RELATED MATERIALS INDICATE THAT ANY OF THESE
ORGANIZATIONS INITIATED, SPONSORED OR ORGANIZED ANY PROTEST (SOCIAL AND/OR
POLITICALLY ORIENTED) WITHIN THE CITY OR MNA? WHICH ONES?

                 _____ YES

                 _____ NO

_____

_____

_____

COMMENTS

G. DOES THE CASE STUDIES, AND OTHER RELATED MATERIALS, INDICATE THE DEGREE OF
INTERACTION AND COOPERATION AMONG THESE ORGANIZATIONS?

                 _____ STRONG INTERACTION/COOPERATION

                 _____ MILD

                 _____ LOW

COMMENTS

111 THE INDEPENDENT VARIABLES (MEASURES OF THE EXTENT AND CHARACTER OF PARTICI-
PATION)

1. RESIDENT INVOLVEMENT IN THE APPLICATION PERIOD FOR A MODEL CITIES GRANT

A. IN ACCORDANCE WITH THE CASE STUDIES LIST THE ACTORS, THEIR OCCUPATION, COMMUNITY ORGANIZATION AFFILIATION WHO INITIATED INTEREST IN THE MODEL CITIES PROGRAM

ACTOR   OCCUPATION   ORGANIZATION

COMMENTS

B. DIAGRAM THE PROCESS, OR STEPS, FROM THE INITIATION OF INTEREST TO THE ACTUAL MUNICIPAL DECISION TO APPLY FOR THE MODEL CITIES GRANT

COMMENTS

C. WHAT ROLE DID RESIDENTS OF THE MNA PLAY IN THE PRE-APPLICATION PHASE?

_____ NO ROLE

_____ ACTIVE ROLE

_____ CONTROLLING ROLE

COMMENTS

D. ONCE THE CITY DECIDED TO APPLY FOR A MODEL CITIES GRANT, WHICH ACTORS WERE BROUGHT TOGETHER TO WRITE THE APPLICATION?

ACTOR   OCCUPATION   ORGANIZATION   RESIDENT OF MNA?

COMMENTS

E. WHAT ROLE DID THE RESIDENTS OF THE MNA PLAY IN THE WRITE-UP PHASE OF THE APPLICATION?

_____ NO ROLE

_____ ACTIVE ROLE

_____ MILD ROLE

_____ CONTROLLING ROLE

COMMENTS

F. WERE RESIDENTS GIVEN DUE NOTICE THAT THE MUNICIPALITY HAD APPLIED FOR A
    MODEL CITIES GRANT?

                                                _____ YES

                                                _____ NO

G. IF YES, HOW?

                            _____ TOWN MEETINGS

                            _____ RADIO AND TELEVISION

                            _____ NEWSPAPER

                            _____ THROUGH COMMUNITY REPRESENTATIVES

    COMMENTS

2. INDICES OF RESIDENT ACTIVITY FOR REPRESENTATION ON THE CDA BOARD

A. OUTLINE AND/OR DESCRIBE THE ORIGINALLY PROPOSED STRUCTURE OF THE CDA BOARD

    COMMENTS

B. DURING ANY TIME IN THE APPLICATION PERIOD DID ANY RESIDENT(S) OR OTHER
    PERSON(S), AGENCY OR ORGANIZATION VOICE DISSATISFACTION WITH THE PROPOSED
    STRUCTURE (ADMINISTRATIVE AND GOVERNANCE) OF THE MODEL CITIES PROGRAM?

                                                _____ YES

                                                _____ NO

    COMMENTS

C. IF THERE WERE A PROTEST OR REQUEST FOR A CHANGE IN THE PROPOSED ADMINISTRA-
    TIVE AND GOVERNANCE STRUCTURE OF THE MC PROGRAM - LIST THE SPECIFIC CONCERNS
    OF THE RESIDENTS OR THEIR REPRESENTATIVES

    _____

    _____

    _____

    COMMENTS

D. WHAT WAS THE OUTCOME OF THE PROTEST OR REQUEST?

_____ A REVISION IN ACCORDANCE WITH THE RESIDENTS'
        REQUEST

_____ NO REVISION

E. OUTLINE THE SUBSTANCE OF THE REVISION

COMMENTS

F. DURING ANY PHASE SUBSEQUENT TO THE APPLICATION PERIOD, DID THE RESIDENTS OR
    THEIR REPRESENTATIVES INITIATE AND PARTICIPATE IN ANY FORM OF PROTEST OR
    REQUEST A LARGER ROLE ON THE CDA BOARD?

_____ YES

_____ NO

COMMENTS

G. IF YES, LIST THEIR CONCERNS

_____

_____

_____

COMMENTS

H. WERE THERE ANY CHANGES MADE? IF SO, WHAT?

I. WAS THERE A PROCEDURE WHEREBY THE RESIDENTS WERE ABLE TO APPROVE THE FINAL
    GOVERNANCE AND ADMINISTRATIVE STRUCTURE OF THE MODEL CITIES PROGRAM?

_____ YES

_____ NO

COMMENTS

J. DID RESIDENTS APPROVE THE FINAL STRUCTURE OF THE MC PROGRAM?

_____ YES, OVERWHELMINGLY

133

3. RESIDENTS PARTICIPATION IN THE SELECTION OF THE FIRST CDA DIRECTOR

A. LIST THE CANDIDATES CONSIDERED FOR THE POSITION OF CDA DIRECTOR, THEIR OCCUPATION, EDUCATIONAL BACKGROUND, AFFILIATED ORGANIZATION, RESIDENT/NO RESIDENT, ETHNICITY.

ACTOR   OCCUP.   ED.   ORG.   RESIDENT?   ETHNICITY

COMMENTS

B. WAS THERE AN ESTABLISHED PROCESS FOR SELECTING CANDIDATES FOR THE CDA POSITION?

_____ YES

_____ NO

COMMENTS

C. WHICH ACTORS WERE RESPONSIBLE FOR DESIGNING AND ESTABLISHING THE PROCESS?

_____   RESIDENT?   _____

_____   _____

_____   _____

COMMENTS

D. WHAT ROLE DID THE RESIDENTS PLAY IN DESIGNING AND ESTABLISHING THE CDA SELECTION PROCESS?

_____ NO ROLE

_____ ACTIVE ROLE

_____ CONTROLLING ROLE

COMMENTS

E. WHAT SET OF CRITERIA WAS ESTABLISHED FOR THE SELECTION OF THE CDA DIRECTOR?

134

F. WHICH ACTORS ESTABLISHED THESE CRITERIA?

_____   RESIDENT?   _____

_____   _____

_____   _____

G. WHAT ROLE DID THE RESIDENTS PLAY IN PROVIDING INPUT FOR THE CDA SELECTION
    CRITERIA?

                                            _____ NO ROLE

                                            _____ ACTIVE ROLE

                                            _____ MILD ROLE

                                            _____ CONTROLLING ROLE

H. IF THEIR WAS A CHANGE IN DIRECTORSHIP DURING THE PERIOD UNDER STUDY, DID THE
    RESIDENTS PLAY A ROLE IN HIS SELECTION?

                                            _____ NO ROLE

                                            _____ ACTIVE ROLE

                                            _____ MILD ROLE

                                            _____ CONTROLLING ROLE

I. DID THE SELECTED DIRECTOR DEMONSTRATE AND/OR VOICE SYMPATHY FOR THE COMMUNITY
    CONTROL PHILOSOPHY?

                                            _____ STRONG SUPPORTER

                                            _____ MILD

                                            _____ NO

4. RESIDENTS INPUT INTO THE STRUCTURED AND FORMALIZED PREROGATIVES OF THE CDA BOARD

A. DURING THE APPLICATION AND EARLY PLANNING PHASES OF THE PROGRAM, WHICH ACTORS WERE BROUGHT TOGETHER TO DESIGN THE STRUCTURE AND ESTABLISH THE PREROGATIVES OF THE CDA BOARD?

_____   RESIDENT?   _____

_____   _____

_____   _____

COMMENTS

B. WHAT ROLE DID THE RESIDENTS PLAY IN DESIGNING THE STRUCTURE AND ESTABLISHING THE PREROGATIVES OF THE CDA BOARD?

_____ NO ROLE

_____ ACTIVE ROLE

_____ MILD ROLE

_____ CONTROLLING ROLE

COMMENTS

C. WITHIN THE ESTABLISHED STRUCTURE, WHAT WERE THE FORMAL PREROGATIVES OF THE RESIDENTS?

COMMENTS

D. IS THERE A RESIDENT STRUCTURE SEPARATE FROM THE CDA BOARD?

_____ YES

_____ NO

COMMENTS

E. IF YES, WHY AND HOW DID IT EVOLVE?

COMMENTS

136

F. WHAT ARE THE RESIDENTS' PREROGATIVES IN THIS STRUCTURE?

    COMMENTS

G. WHAT WAS THE RESIDENTS' ROLE IN ESTABLISHING THE PREROGATIVES OF THE
    REQUIRED CITIZEN STRUCTURE OF THE MC PROGRAM?

                                              _____ NO ROLE

                                              _____ ACTIVE ROLE

                                              _____ MILD

                                              _____ CONTROLLING

    COMMENTS

H. WHAT ARE THE RESIDENTS' PREROGATIVES IN THIS STRUCTURE?

    COMMENTS

5. STRUCTURE AND COMPOSITION OF CDA BOARD

A. DIAGRAM THE STRUCTURE OF THE CDA BOARD

    COMMENTS

B. LIST THE MEMBERS OF THE CDA BOARD, OCCUPATION, ETHNICITY, RESIDENT OR NON-
    RESIDENT?

    ACTOR   OCCUPATION   ETHNICITY   RESIDENT?

C. WHAT PERCENTAGE OF THE BOARD ARE ETHNIC MINORITY MEMBERS?

    COMMENTS

6. REPRESENTATIVENESS OF THE RESIDENT STRUCTURE OF THE NEIGHBORHOOD CONSTITUENCY

A. THROUGH WHAT PROCESS WAS THE RESIDENTS OF THE CITIZEN PARTICIPATION STRUCTURE

SELECTED?

_____ APPOINTED BY THE MAYOR

_____ SELECTED BY ELECTION IN THE MNA

_____ APPOINTED BY REPRESENTATIVE ORGANIZATIONS IN THE MNA

_____ OTHER

COMMENTS

B. WITHIN THE CASE STUDIES AND RELATED MATERIALS WHAT ARE THE LOCAL JUDGEMENTS
   (FROM STAFF, RESIDENTS, NEWSPAPERS, ETC.) OF THE REPRESENTATIVENESS OF THE
   RESIDENTS STRUCTURE IN THE MC PROGRAM?

_____ VERY REPRESENTATIVE

_____ MINIMALLY REPRESENTATIVE

_____ NOT REPRESENTATIVE

COMMENTS

7. EXTENT AND NATURE OF TRAINING AND TECHNICAL ASSISTANCE TO RESIDENT PARTICI-
   PATION STRUCTURE

A. WERE THE RESIDENTS ADVISED OF THEIR RIGHTS TO TRAINING AND TECHNICAL
   ASSISTANCE UNDER THE MODEL CITIES PROGRAM?

_____ YES

_____ NO

COMMENTS

B. IF YES, WHO CONTRACTED THE STAFF TO PROVIDE T. & T.A.

_____ RESIDENTS

_____ CDA DIRECTOR

COMMENTS

C. WAS THE T & T.A. STAFF FOR RESIDENTS REGULARLY EMPLOYED PROFESSIONAL STAFF
   OF THE CDA OR WERE THEY CONTRACTED EXCLUSIVELY TO PROVIDE T & T.A. TO THE
   RESIDENT STRUCTURE?

138

_____ CDA STAFF

_____ EXCLUSIVELY

COMMENTS

D. WHERE POSSIBLE, LIST ACTIVITIES AND SERVICES PERFORMED BY T & T.A. STAFF

COMMENTS

8. EXTENT OF INFORMATION FLOW FROM CDA ADMINISTRATIVE UNITS TO RESIDENT STRUCTURE

A. IS THERE AN ESTABLISHED PROCEDURE WHICH INSURES THAT THE RESIDENT STRUCTURE HAVE SUFFICIENT INFORMATION ABOUT ANY MATTER TO BE DECIDED IN A SUFFICIENT PERIOD OF TIME?

_____ YES

_____ NO

COMMENTS

B. DOES THE STAFF IN GENERAL FEEL THAT THIS PROCEDURE HAS BEEN EFFICIENT?

_____ YES

_____ NO

COMMENTS

C. DO THE RESIDENTS IN GENERAL FEEL THAT THIS PROCEDURE HAS BEEN EFFICIENT?

_____ YES

_____ NO

COMMENTS

9. EXTENT AND/OR DEGREE OF PROFESSIONAL REACTION AND/OR COOPERATION WITH RESIDENT STRUCTURE

A. DOES THE CASE STUDIES AND RELATED MATERIALS INDICATE THAT THE PROFESSIONAL STAFF:

_____ STRONGLY SUPPORTED COOPERATION WITH THE RESIDENT STRUCTURE

_____ GENERALLY SUPPORTED COOPERATION WITH THE RESIDENT STRUCTURE

_____ MILDLY SUPPORTED COOPERATION WITH THE RESIDENT STRUCTURE

COMMENTS

10. DEPENDENT VARIABLES (MEASURES OF CONTROL)

1. DEGREE OF INFLUENCE (AUTHORITY) OF RESIDENT STRUCTURE IN THE HIRING OF THE MODEL CITIES PERSONNEL

_____ NO AUTHORITY

_____ SHARED AUTHORITY

_____ MILD AUTHORITY

_____ COMPLETE AUTHORITY

COMMENTS

2. DEGREE OF AUTHORITY OF RESIDENTS' STRUCTURE IN THE FIRING OF MODEL CITIES PERSONNEL

_____ NO AUTHORITY

_____ SHARED AUTHORITY

_____ MILD AUTHORITY

_____ COMPLETE AUTHORITY

COMMENTS

3. DEGREE OF AUTHORITY OF RESIDENT STRUCTURE IN THE ALLOCATION OF MODEL CITIES BUDGET

_____ NO AUTHORITY

_____ SHARED AUTHORITY

_____ MILD AUTHORITY

_____ COMPLETE AUTHORITY

COMMENTS

4. DEGREE OF RESIDENTS AUTHORITY IN THE INITIATION OF MODEL CITIES PROGRAMS

                                            _____ NO AUTHORITY

                                            _____ SHARED AUTHORITY

                                            _____ MILD AUTHORITY

                                            _____ COMPLETE AUTHORITY

COMMENTS

5. DEGREE OF RESIDENTS AUTHORITY IN THE DESIGN OF MODEL CITIES PROGRAMS

                                            _____ NO AUTHORITY

                                            _____ SHARED AUTHORITY

                                            _____ MILD AUTHORITY

                                            _____ COMPLETE AUTHORITY

COMMENTS

6. DEGREE OF RESIDENTS AUTHORITY IN THE OPERATION OF MODEL CITIES PROGRAMS

                                            _____ NO AUTHORITY

                                            _____ SHARED AUTHORITY

                                            _____ MILD AUTHORITY

                                            _____ COMPLETE AUTHORITY

COMMENTS

SELECTED BIBLIOGRAPHY

Aleshire, Robert A., "Power to the People? An Assessment of the Community
1972   Action and Model Cities Experiences", Public Administration Review,
        Vol. XXXII, September, 428-444.

Altshuler, Alan A., Community Control: The Black Demand for Participation in
1970   Large American Cities, New York Pegasus.

Anton, Thomas, "Power, Pluralism and Local Politics", Administrative Science
1963   Quarterly, VII, 448-457.

Arnstein, Sherry R., "Ladder of Citizen Participation", Journal of the American
1969   Institute of Planners, XXV, 216-224.

Arnstein, Sherry R. (as told to), "Maximum Feasible Manipulation in Philadelphia:
1970   What the Power Structure Did to Us", City, V. 4, N. 3.

Arnstein, Sherry R. and Fox, Dan, "Developments, Dynamics and Dilemmas", Internal
1968   Staff Memorandum on Citizen Participation in the Model Cities Program,
        HUD, August.

Ascher, Charles S., "The Participation of Private Individuals in Administrative
1970   Tasks", paper delivered at International Academy of Comparative Law,
        Pescara, Italy.

Ash, Joan, Planning with People, U.S.A., London: Ministry of Housing and Local
1965   Government.

Austin, David M., "The Black Civic Volunteer Leader: A New Era in Voluntarism",
1970   Harriet Lowenstein Goldstein Series, Issue N. 5; The Volunteer in
        America, The Florence Heller Graduate School for Advanced Studies in
        Social Welfare, Waltham, Massachusetts: Brandeis University.

_____, "Resident Participation: Political Mobilization or Organizational
1972   Co-optation?" Public Administration Review, Vol. XXXII, September.

Babcock, R., and Bosselman, F., "Citizen Participation: A Suburban Suggestion
1967   for the Central City", Law and Contemporary Problems, XXXIII, 220-231.

Baida, Robert, "Local Control Essential in Model Cities Program", speech re-
1970   ported in HUD News, July 18, 1969.

Banfield, Edward, The Unheavenly City: The Nature and Future of Our Urban
1968   Crisis, Little Brown and Company.

Barshay, Shirley, One Meaning of "Citizen Participation": A Report on the First
1969   Year of Model Cities in Oakland, California, prepared under a grant
        from the Office of Economic Opportunity, Western Region.

Bell, Wendell, and Force, Maryanne, "Urban Neighborhood Types and Participation
1965   in Formal Associations", American Sociological Review, XXI, 25-34.

142

Binstock, Robert; Ely, Katherine (eds), <u>The Politics of the Powerless</u>, Winthrop
    1971   Publishers, Cambridge, Massachusetts.

Bike, E., "Citizen Participation in Renewal", <u>Journal of Housing</u>, XXIII, 18-21.
    1966

Boone, Richard, "Reflections on Citizen Participation and the Economic Opportun-
    1970   ity Act", paper prepared for the National Academy of Public Administra-
           tion.

Brignac, Ronald L., "Public Housing Official Reacts to Citizen Participation
    1969   Menages with One-Man Drama", <u>Journal of Housing</u>, XXVI, 604-605.

Buchanan, Jeffrey D., "Urban Renewal in DeSoto-Carr: Citizen Participation
    1970   Comes of Age", <u>Urban Law Annual</u>, St. Louis, Washington University, 103-
           132.

Burke, Edmund M., "Citizen Participation in Renewal", <u>Journal of Housing</u>, XXXIII,
    1966   18-25.

_____, "Citizen Participation Strategies", <u>Journal of the American Institute</u>
    1968 <u>of Planners</u>, XXXIV, 287-294.

Cahn, Edward S., and Cahn, Jean C., "The War on Poverty: A Civilian Perspective",
    1964   <u>Yale Law Journal</u>, 1317-1352.

_____, "Citizen Participation", in Spiegel, Hans B. C., <u>Citizen Participa-</u>
    1968 <u>tion in Urban Development</u>, 211-224.

_____ (eds), <u>Citizen Participation: Effecting Community Change</u>, Praeger
    1971   Publishers, New York.

Campbell, Louise, "Paul Ylvisaker: The Art of the Impossible", <u>City</u>, III, No. 2.
    1969

Clark, Kenneth (principal investigator), "Youth in the Ghetto: A Study of the
    1964   Consequence of Powerlessness", Orans Press.

Cloward, Richard; Ohlin, Lloyd, <u>Delinquency and Opportunity</u>, Free Press, New York.
    1960

Cloward, Richard; Piven, Frances, Fox, <u>Regulating the Poor: Functions of Public</u>
    1971   <u>Welfare</u>, Basic Books, Inc., New York.

_____, "Black Control of Cities", <u>New Republic</u>, September 30.

Crain, Robert, and Rosenthal, Donald, "Community Status and a Dimension of Social
    1967   Decision-Making", <u>American Sociological Review</u>, XXXII, 132-135.

Cunningham, James, <u>The Resurgent Neighborhood</u>, Notre Dame: Fides Publishers, Inc.
    1965

Dahl, Robert A., "The Analysis of Influence in Local Communities", in <u>Social</u>
    1960   <u>Science and Community Action</u>, edited by Charles Adrian, East Lansing:

Institute for Community Development and Services, Michigan State University.

Davies, J. Clarence, III, Neighborhood Groups and Urban Renewal, New York:
1966   Columbia University Press.

Davis, James W., and Dolbeare, Kenneth M., Little Groups of Neighbors, Chicago:
1968   Markham Publishing Company.

Davis, Lloyd, "With Citizen Participation: New Haven Has Neighborhood Rehab
1965   Success Story", Journal of Housing, XXII, 132-135.

DeHuzar, George B., Practical Application of Democracy, New York: Harper and
1945   Bros.

Denhardt, Robert, "Organizational Citizenship and Personal Freedom", Public
1968   Administration Review, XXVIII, 47-53.

Denise, Paul, "Some Participation Innovations", in Spiegel, Hans B. C.,
1969   Citizen Participation in Urban Development.

Donovan, John C., The Politics of Poverty, New York: Pegasus.
1967

Edelston, Harold, and Kolodner, Fern, "Are the Poor Capable of Planning for
1967   Themselves?", address before the National Association of Social
        Welfare Conference, Dallas.

Fredrickson, George (ed.), Politics, Public Administration and Neighborhood
1972   Control, Chandler Publishers, San Francisco.

Grier, William H.; Cobbs, Price, M., Black Rage, Bantam Books, Inc.
1968

Gross, Bertram, "Friendly Facism: A Model for America", Social Policy, Vol. 1,
1970   No. 4, 44-53.

Hallman, Howard, Community Control: A Study of Community Corporations and
1969   Neighborhood Boards, Washington, Washington Center for Metropolitan
        Studies.

_____, "Federally Financed Citizen Participation", paper prepared for the
1970   National Academy of Public Administration.

Hamilton, Randy, "Citizen Participation: A Mildly Restrained View", Public
1969   Management, LI, No. 7, 6-8.

Hayes, Frederick, "Text of Hayes Memorandum on Consultant Contracts", The New
1970   York Times, July 3, p. 3.

Herman, M. Justin, "Renewal Official Responds to Citizen Participation State-
1969   ments of Messrs. Burke and Rutledge", Journal of Housing, XXVI, No.
        11.

144

Hunter College, Department of Urban Affairs, The Citizen Planner Speaks:
1969   Citizen Participation in the New York City Model Cities Planning
        Process, Hunter College, Department of Urban Affairs, New York.

Hyman, Herbert H., "Planning with Citizens: Two Styles", JAIP, 105-112.
1969

Kaplan, Harold, Urban Renewal Politics: Slum Clearance in Newark, New York:
1963   Columbia University Press.

Kaplan, Marshall, "The Role of the Planner in Urban Areas: Modest, Intuitive
1968   Claims for Advocacy", paper presented at the National Association
        of Social Welfare Conference, New York City, May.

_____, "HUD Model Cities - Planning System", paper prepared for the
1970   National Academy of Public Administration.

Kaufman, Herbert, "Administrative Decentralization and Political Power", Public
1969   Administration Review, XXIX.

Keyes, Langley, Rehabilitation Planning Game: A Study in the Diversity of
1969   Neighborhood, Cambridge: M.I.T. Press.

Kohn, Sherwood, Experiment in Planning an Urban High School: The Baltimore
1969   Cigarette Report, Educational Facilities Laboratories, New York.

Kotler, Milton, Neighborhood Government: Local Foundations of Political Life,
1969   Indianapolis, Indiana: The Bobbs-Merrill Company.

_____, "Two Essays on the Neighborhood Corporation", in Urban American:
1967   Goals and Problems, edited by Subcommittee on Urban Affairs, Joint
        Economic Committee, U.S. Congress, Washington, D.C.: Government
        Printing Office.

Kramer, Ralph M., Participation of the Poor, Englewood Cliffs, New Jersey:
1969   Prentice-Hall, Inc.

Larrabee, Kent R., "Highway Project Planning with Local Citizens", remarks at
1970   Highway Management Institute, University of Mississippi, March 13,
        1970.

Lewis, Gerda, "Citizen Participation in Renewal Surveyed", JAIP, XVI, 80-87.
1959

Levitan, Sar, The Design of Federal Antipoverty Strategy, University of Michigan
1967   and Wayne State University, Institute of Labor and Industrial Rela-
        tions.

Lightfoot, Claude, Ghetto Rebellion to Black Liberation, International Publishers
1968   Company, Inc.

Lindsay, John V., "A Plan for Neighborhood Government for New York City", City
1970   of New York.

Lipsky, Michael, "Toward a Theory of Street-Level Bureaucracy", paper delivered
    1969   at the American Political Science Association, New York City,
            September, 1969.

Mann, Seymour Z., "Participation in Model Cities Planning", paper presented at
    1969   the 75th National Conference on Government, National Municipal League,
            Philadelphia, Pa.

_____, "Participation of the Poor and Model Cities in New York", paper
    1970   prepared for the National Academy of Public Administration.

Mann, Seymour Z. (ed.), Proceedings of National Conference on Advocacy and
    1970   Pluralistic Planning, Urban Research Center, Department of Urban
            Affairs, Hunter College, New York.

Marcuse, Peter, Tenant Participation - For What?, Working Paper, The Urban
    1970   Institute, Washington, D.C.

Marris, Peter, and Martin Rein, Dilemma of Social Reform, London: Atherton,
    1967

Mathews, Vincent, Citizen Participation: An Analytical Study of the Literature,
    1968   Catholic University, Washington, D.C.

Metropolitan Applied Research Center (MARC), A Relevant War Against Poverty,
    1968   New York.

_____, "The Future of Maximum Feasible Participation", unpublished paper
    1968   delivered at the Alumni Meeting, Columbia University School of Social
            Work, New York.

Mittenthal, Stephen D., "The Power Pendulum: An Examination of Power and
    1970   Planning in the Low-Income Community", Ph.D. Dissertation, Columbia
            University, New York.

Mittenthal, Stephen D., and Spiegel, Hans B. C., Urban Confrontation: City
    1970   Versus Neighborhood in Model City Planning Process, New York:
            Institute of Urban Environment, Columbia University.

Mogulof, Melvin, "Coalition to Adversary: Citizen Participation in Three
    1969   Federal Programs", JAIP, XXXV, 225-232.

_____, Citizen Participation: A Review and Commentary on Federal Policies
    1970(a) and Practices, Part I working paper for the Urban Institute,
            Washington, D.C.

_____, Citizen Participation: The Local Perspective, Part II, working
    1970(b) paper for the Urban Institute, Washington, D.C.

Moynihan, Daniel P., Maximum Feasible Misunderstanding: Community Action in
    1969   the War Against Poverty, New York, Free Press.

Moynihan, Daniel P. (ed.), Toward a National Urban Policy, New York: Basic Books.
    1970

Office of Economic Opportunity, Community Action Guide, Washington, D.C.: OEO.
    1965

_____, Community Action Memorandum 80 - Designation and Recognition of
    1968(a) Community Action Agencies, Under the 1967 Amendments.

_____, Community Action Memorandum 81 - The Organization of Community
    1968(b) Action Boards and Committees under the 1967 Amendments.

_____, OEO Instruction #6907-1, Restrictions on Political Activities,
    1968(c) Community Action Program, September 6, 1968.

_____, OEO Instruction #6320-1, The Mission of the Community Action Agency,
    1970   November 16, 1970.

Office of Voluntary Action, National Center for Voluntary Action - Office of
    1970   Voluntary Action, as of November, 1970, Washington, D.C.

Peattie, Lisa R., "Reflections in Advocacy Planning," JAIP, XXXIV, 80-88.
    1968

Perloff, Harvey, and Hansen, Royce, "Inner City and a New Politics", in Urban
    1967   America: Goals and Problems, edited by Subcommittee on Urban
            Affairs, Joint Economic Committee, U.S. Congress, Washington, D.C.,
            Government Printing Office.

Pinkney, Alphonso, Black Americans, Prentice Hall, Inc., Englewood Cliffs, New
    1969   Jersey.

Piven, Frances, "Participation of Residents in Neighborhood Community Action
    1966   Programs", Social Work, V. 1, N. 1.

Pomeroy, Hugh R., "The Planning Process and Public Participation", in An
    1953   Approach to Urban Planning, edited by Gerald Breese and Dorothy E.
            Whiteman, Princeton: Princeton University Press.

President's Task Force on Model Cities, Model Cities: A Step Toward New
    1970   Federalism, Washington, D.C., Government Printing Office.

Rein, Martin, "Social Planning: The Search for Legitimacy", JAIP, XXXV, 233-244.
    1969

Robinson, David Z. (ed.), Report of HUD/NYU Summer Study on Citizen Involvement
    1968   in Urban Affairs, report to the U.S. Department of Housing and Urban
            Development, Washington, D.C.; New York: NYU.

Rosenbaum, Allen, "Participation Programs & Politics -- The Federal Impact on
    1970   the Metropolis", paper presented at the American Political Science
            Association, Los Angeles, California.

Rossi, Peter, "Theory in Community Organization", in Social Science and Community
    1960   Action, edited by Charles Adrian, East Lansing, Michigan: Institute
            for Community Development & Service.

Rossi, Peter, and Dentler, Robert A., The Politics of Urban Renewal: The
1961   Chicago Findings, New York: Free Press.

Seaver, Robert, "The Dilemma of Citizen Participation", Pratt Planning Papers,
1966   N. 4, 6-10.

Siegal, Roberta, "Citizen Committees - Advice vs. Consent", Trans-Action, 47-52.
1967

Smith, David Horton; Reddy, Richard D.; and Baldwin, Burt R., "Types of
1972   Voluntary Action: A Definitional Essay", in Review of Voluntary
        Action Theory and Research, V. 1, edited by Smith, D. H., et al,
        Beverly Hills, California: Sage Publications.

Soysel, Mumtaz (ed.), Public Relations in Administration: The Influence of the
1966   Public on the Operation of Public Administration, Brussels,
        International Institute of Administrative Science.

Spiegel, Hans B. C., "Human Considerations in Urban Renewal", University of
1968(b) Toronto Law Journal, XVIII, 308-18.

Spiegel, Hans B. C. (ed.), Citizen Participation in Urban Development: Concepts
1968(a) and Issues, Washington, D.C." NTL Institute for Applied Behavioral
        Science.

_____, Citizen Participation in Urban Development: Cases and Programs,
1969(b) Washington, D.C.: NTL Institute for Applied Behavioral Science.

Spiegel, Hans B. C., and Alicea, Victor G., "The Trade-Off Strategy in Community
1969   Research", Social Science Quarterly, L, 598-603.

Spiegel, Hans B. C., and Mittenthal, Stephen D., Neighborhood Power and Control:
1968   Implications for Urban Planning, report to the U.S. Department of
        Housing and Urban Development, Washington, D.C.; New York: Institute
        of Urban Environment, Columbia University.

Starr, Roger, "An Attack on Poverty: Historical Perspective", in Urban America:
1967   Goals and Problems, edited by Subcommittee on Urban Affairs, Joint
        Economic Committee, U.S. Congress, Washington, D.C.: Government
        Printing Office.

Sundquist, James L., Making Federalism Work, The Brookings Institution, Boston,
1969   Massachusetts.

_____ (ed.), On Fighting Poverty, New York: Basic Books.
1969

"Symposium on Alienation, Decentralization and Participation", January/ February,
1969   1969, Public Administrative Review, XXIX, 2-64.

Taylor, Ralph C., Speech to the National Association on Housing and Redevelopment
1968   Officials, Minneapolis, September 28, 1968.

"Tenant-Management Issues", Journal of Housing, V. 27, N. 10, 534-543.

Unger, Sherman, "Citizen Participation - A Challenge to HUD and the Community",
1970   Urban Lawyer, V. 2, 29-39.

U.S. Department of Health, Education and Welfare, Head Start Child Development
1967   Program: A Manual of Policies and Instructions, Office of Child
        Development.

_____, Parents as Partners in Department Programs for Children and Youth,
1968   report to the Secretary of HEW by the Task Force on Parent
        Participation.

_____, Memorandum to Chief State School Officers: Advisory Statement on
1970(a) Development of Policy Parental Involvement in Title I, ESEA Projects,
        Washington, D.C.

_____, Transmittal Notice: Head Start Policy Manual 70.2, August 10, 1970.
1970(b)

_____, Project Guide for Areawide Comprehensive Health Planning, Public
1970(c) Health Service.

_____, "Joint HUD-OEO Citizen Participation Policy for Model Cities Programs",
1970(d) CDA Letter #108.

U.S. Department of Housing and Urban Development, Program Guide: Model
1966   Neighborhoods in Demonstration Cities, Washington, D.C.

_____, Citizen Participation, CDA Letter #3.
1967(a)

_____, "Draft Guidelines for the Social Service Program," Housing Assistance
1967(b) Administration, Washington, D.C.

_____, Content Analysis of First Round Model Cities Applications, Washington,
1968(a) D.C.

_____, Citizen Participation Today, Proceedings at a Staff Conference,
1968(b) Region IV, Chicago, Illinois.

_____, The Model Cities Program: A History and Analysis of Planning Process
1969(a) in Three Cities, prepared by Marshall Kaplan, Gans, and Kahn,
        Washington, D.C.: GPO.

_____, Urban Renewal Handbook, LPA Administration, Chapter 5, Washington,
1969(b) D.C.

_____, Comprehensive Planning Assistance Handbook, V. 1, MD 6041.1,
1969(c) Chapter 61, Washington, D.C.

_____, Citizen and Business Participation in Urban Affairs: A Bibliography,
1970(a) Washington, D.C.

_____, Workable Program for Community Improvement, Washington, D.C.
  1970(b)

_____, "Circular: Appointment of Tenants as Local Housing Authority
  1970(c) Commissioners", Washington, D.C.

_____, "Joint HUD-OEO Citizen Participation Policy for Model Cities Program",
  1970(d) CDA Letter #108.

U.S. Department of Transportation, Policy and Procedure Memorandum, Transmittal
  1969   162, Federal Highway Administration, November 24.

Van Til, Jon, and Van Til, Sally Bould, "Citizen Participation in Social Policy:
  1970   End of Cycle?", Social Problems, XVII, 313-323.

Verba, Sidney, "Democratic Participation", The Annals, II, 53-78.
  1967

Voluntary Action News, V. 1, N. 2, November, 1970, National Center for Voluntary
  1970   Action, 1735 Eye Street NW, Washington, D.C.

Yette, Samuel, The Choice: The Issue of Black Survival in America, G. P.
  1969   Putnam's Sons, New York.

Warren, Roland, "Model Cities First Round: Politics, Planning and Participation",
  1969   JAIP, XXXV, 242-252.

_____, Purposive Change and the Social Construction of Reality, paper
  1972   submitted at the annual meeting of the Society of Social Problems,
          August.

_____ (ed.), Politics and the Ghetto, Atherton Press.
  1972

Watson, Norman V., "The Role of Tenants in Public Housing", remarks at the
  1970   Conference of the National Tenants Organization by HUD Acting
          Assistant Secretary, Winston Salem, N.C., November 21.

Weaver, Robert C., Speech to Family Service Association of America, New York
  1961   City, November 13.

White House News Release, Executive Order Prescribing Arrangements for the
  1969   Structure and Conduct of a National Program for Voluntary Action,
          May 26.

Williams, Junius W., "The Impact of Citizen Participation", paper prepared for
  1970   the National Academy of Public Administration.

Wilson, James Q., "Planning and Politics: Citizen Participation in Urban
  1963(a) Renewal", JAIP, XXXIX, 242-249.

_____, "The Citizen in the Renewal Process", Journal of Housing, XX, 622-
  1963(b) 627.

Wood, Robert C., "Science: The Urban Witch", unpublished paper delivered at the
1968   Second Annual Symposium of the American Society of Cybernetics,
         October, 1968, Washington, D.C.

_____, "Citizen Participation in the Administrative Process", address to
1968   the National Conference of the American Society of Public Administra-
         tion, March 28, 1968, Boston, Massachusetts.

_____, "A Call for Return to Community", Public Management, L1.
1969

Zurcher, Louis A., Poverty Warriors: The Human Experience of Planned Social
1970   Intervention, Austin, Texas, University of Texas Press.